19th Joint ACL-ISO Workshop on Interoperable Semantic Annotation (ISA-19)

Nancy, France
20 June 2023

ISBN: 978-1-7138-9054-6

Printed from e-media with permission by:

Curran Associates, Inc.
57 Morehouse Lane
Red Hook, NY 12571

Printed with permission by Curran Associates, Inc. (2024)

Association for Computational Linguistics
209 N. Eighth Street
Stroudsburg, Pennsylvania 18360

Phone: 1-570-476-8006
Fax: 1-570-476-0860

acl@aclweb.org

Additional copies of this publication are available from:

Curran Associates, Inc.
57 Morehouse Lane
Red Hook, NY 12571 USA
Phone: 845-758-0400
Fax: 845-758-2633
Email: curran@proceedings.com
Web: www.proceedings.com

ISA-19

The 19th Joint ACL - ISO Workshop on Interoperable Semantic Annotation

Proceedings of the Workshop

June 20, 2023

at IWCS 2023
Nancy, France

Message from the Organisers

Welcome to the proceedings of ISA-19, the nineteenth edition in the series of Joint ACL – ISO Workshops on Interoperable Semantic Annotation. This year the workshop is organised within the context of the 2023 International Conference on Computational Semantics (IWCS 2023) in Nancy, France. We thank the IWCS 2023 organisers for their support, taking care of a variety of practical matters that would otherwise not have been easy to deal with.

The accepted papers that were submitted to the ISA-19 workshop are presented in these proceedings in the same order as their presentations at the workshop.

In order to maximally support prospective authors in submitting papers on recent research, we worked with a late submission deadline, a very short review period, and a longer period for revising and optimising the accepted papers. We are very thankful that the members of the Programme Committee complied with this strategy and managed to submit thorough reviews in the very short period that they had. Needless to say that without their efforts it would not be possible to have the workshop. Thank you! We also thank the authors of the accepted papers for revising their contributions according to the proposed time schedule, taking the review comments into account and producing a range of interesting papers.

The ISA-19 organisers,

Harry Bunt, Nancy Ide, Kiyong Lee, Volha Petukhova, James Pustejovsky, and Laurent Romary

Organizing Committee

Organisers:

- Harry Bunt (chair)
- Nancy Ide
- Kiyong Lee
- Volha Petukhova
- James Pustejovsky
- Laurent Romary

Programme Committee:

- Jan Alexandersson
- Johan Bos
- Harry Bunt
- Stergios Chatzykiriakidis
- Jae-Woong Choe
- Robin Cooper
- Rodolfo Delmonte
- David DeVault
- Simon Dobnik
- Jens Edlund
- Alex Fang
- Robert Gaizauskas
- Koiti Hasida
- Nancy Ide
- Elisabetta Jezek
- Nikhil Krishnaswamy
- Kiyong Lee
- Paul Mc Kevitt
- Philippe Muller
- Rainer Osswald
- Catherine Pelachaud
- Guy Perrier
- Volha Petukhova
- Massimo Poesio
- Andrei Popescu-Belis
- Laurent Prévot
- Stephen Pulman
- Matthew Purver
- James Pustejovsky
- Laurent Romary
- Purificação Silvano
- Matthew Stone
- Thorsten Trippel
- University of Tübingen
- Carl Vogel
- Menno van Zaanen
- Annie Zaenen
- Heike Zinsmeister

Table of Contents

Conference Program

09:10–10:05 Session 1

09:10–09:30 *The DARPA Wikidata Overlay: Wikidata as an ontology for natural language processing*
Elizabeth Spaulding, Kathryn Conger, Anatole Gershman, Rosario Uceda-Sosa, Susan Windisch Brown, James Pustejovsky, Peter Anick and Martha Palmer

09:45–10:05 *Semantic annotation of Common Lexis Verbs of Contact in Bulgarian*
Maria Todorova

10:40–12:15 Session 2

10:40–11:00 *Appraisal Theory and the Annotation of Speaker-Writer Engagement*
Min Dong and Alex Fang

11:15–11:35 *metAMoRphosED, a graphical editor for Abstract Meaning Representation*
Johannes Heinecke and Maria Boritchev

11:35–11:55 *Personal noun detection for German*
Carla Sökefeld, Melanie Andresen, Johanna Binnewitt and Heike Zinsmeister

11:55–12:15 *ISO 24617-2 on a cusp of languages*
Krzysztof Hwaszcz, Marcin Oleksy, Aleksandra Domogała and Jan Wieczorek

14:00–14:40 Session 3

14:00–14:20 *Towards Referential Transparent Annotations of Quantified Noun Phrases*
Andy Luecking

14:20–14:40 *The compositional semantics of QuantML annotations*
Harry Bunt

15:30–16:25 Session 4

15:30–15:50 *An Abstract Specification of VoxML as an Annotation Language*
Kiyong Lee, Nikhil Krishnaswamy and James Pustejovsky

16:05–16:25 *How Good is Automatic Segmentation as a Multimodal Discourse Annotation Aid?*
Corbyn Terpstra, Ibrahim Khebour, Mariah Bradford, Brett Wisniewski, Nikhil Krishnaswamy and Nathaniel Blanchard

The DARPA Wikidata Overlay: Wikidata as an ontology for natural language processing

Elizabeth Spaulding[1], **Kathryn Conger**[1], **Anatole Gershman**[2], **Rosario Uceda-Sosa**[3], **Susan Windisch Brown**[1], **James Pustejovsky**[4], **Peter Anick**[4] and **Martha Palmer**[1]

[1]University of Colorado Boulder, [2]Language Technologies Institute, Carnegie Mellon University, [3]IBM Research, T.J.Watson, [4]Brandeis University

{elizabeth.spaulding,kathryn.conger,susan.brown,martha.palmer}@colorado.edu, anatoleg@andrew.cmu.edu, rosariou@us.ibm.com, {pustejovsky,panick}@brandeis.edu

Abstract

With 102,530,067 items currently in its crowd-sourced knowledge base, Wikidata provides NLP practitioners a unique and powerful resource for inference and reasoning over real-world entities. However, because Wikidata is very entity focused, *events* and *actions* are often labeled with eventive nouns (e.g., the process of diagnosing a person's illness is labeled "diagnosis"), and the typical participants in an event are not described or linked to that event concept (e.g., the medical professional or patient). Motivated by a need for an adaptable, comprehensive, domain-flexible ontology for information extraction, including identifying the roles entities are playing in an event, we present a curated subset of Wikidata in which events have been enriched with PropBank roles. To enable richer narrative understanding between events from Wikidata concepts, we have also provided a comprehensive mapping from temporal Qnodes and Pnodes to the Allen Interval Temporal Logic relations.

1 Introduction

An ontology is a necessary framework for practical system representation of domain-specific world knowledge. However, since we each perceive the world somewhat differently, and different domains require access to varying levels of granularity, a unique, universal ontology is not a realistic goal. The biomedical portal[1] alone lists 1213 different biomedical ontologies. The largest structured repository of knowledge about world entities is Wikidata (Vrandečić and Krötzsch, 2014), but, as should be expected from any collective knowledge repository, it has many inconsistencies, circular subclass links, and partially overlapping concepts and gaps. Since every practical project designed for a specific task needs a consistent ontology, our challenge is to provide a common, mutually agreed upon vocabulary that speeds up the process of incorporating new domains or evolving existing ones by automatically leveraging existing knowledge bases, such as Wikidata.

We introduce the DARPA Wikidata Overlay (DWD Overlay), a curated subset of Wikidata enriched with PropBank (Kingsbury and Palmer, 2002) roles. We chose Wikidata as our primary resource for ontological concepts because of its extensive coverage of concepts, its linking of those concepts to each other, and the ability to contribute additional concepts to the database as needed. Importantly, Wikidata concepts are linked to relevant Wikipedia entries, a distinct advantage for NLP applications concerned with current events. We turned to PropBank as our source of participant roles because of its wide coverage of verbs and eventive nouns that we could easily match to Wikidata concepts and because its roles could be represented as both broad, general roles (e.g., ARG0, ARG1) and as more event-specific (e.g., attacker, victim). Further, to enable richer narrative understanding between events, we have provided a comprehensive mapping from temporal Qnodes and Pnodes to the Allen Interval Temporal Logic relations (Allen, 1983, 1984). While Wikidata is a multilingual project, and PropBank is a language-independent semantic description, both resources use a mainly English interface and semantic roles from resources like PropBank can be, to some degree, language-specific (Burchardt et al., 2006).

The overlay is currently hosted in a JSON format[2], designed to give users the ability to browse concepts and easily ingest the ontology structure into their computing applications. We hope that by establishing a robust and accurate mapping be-

[1]https://bioportal.bioontology.org/ontologies

[2]https://github.com/e-spaulding/xpo

Proceedings of the 19th Joint ACL - ISO Workshop on Interoperable Semantic Annotation, pages 1–10
June 20, 2023. ©2023 Association for Computational Linguistics

tween PropBank and Wikidata, we enable the usage of well-established NLP methods for event extraction using PropBank combined with the inference power and massive coverage of Wikidata.

2 Background and Related Work

Wikidata[3] is a large, crowd-sourced knowledge base. Each item in Wikidata refers to a either a concept ("president") or a real-world instantiation of a concept ("Joe Biden"), and is called a *Qnode*. Qnodes are connected to one another via *Pnodes*, which represent the relation in <*subject, relation, object*> triples in Wikidata.

The original impetus for using Wikidata to support DARPA programs came from the DARPA AIDA and KAIROS programs, closely followed by DARPA MAA. Each of the aforementioned DARPA programs is described in more detail below, as well the motivation for coming to a consensus on an approach to ontology development that could be quickly adapted to new domains.

Active Interpretation of Disparate Alternatives (AIDA), now completed, aimed at the organization of natural language news and social network information into competing, alternative hypotheses (narratives) about events and situations. AIDA systems integrated multi-modal knowledge elements into a common semantic representation suitable for hypothesis generation. Task Area 1 (TA1) performers applied cutting-edge NLP techniques to extract and co-refer knowledge elements from streaming text, images and videos, producing entries in a knowledge base (KB) for each input document. The program goals originally included the challenging restriction of TA2's and TA3's performing their tasks without access to raw input data. Without consulting the original TA1 inputs, TA2 performers link together entity and event entries from individual documents into a unified KB using cross-document co-reference techniques. The TA1's could provide TA2's the names of named entities but could not originally provide TA2's with the lexical items or images for other types of entities. Instead, TA2's passed along type information for entity and event entries from an Ontology. This made the development of a program-wide ontology that all performers could utilize a high priority. TA3 performers then mined the unified TA2 KB for competing hypotheses.

At the outset of the program, AIDA worked on developing an expressive, semantic Program Ontology that could be used by performers to encode and exchange KBs and hypotheses. Midway through the program, the Program Ontology contained hundreds of entity, relation, and event types developed using a data-driven approach inspired by pre-existing knowledge resources. These included previous Linguistic Data Consortium (LDC) annotation efforts, such as ACE (Strassel and Mitchell, 2003; Doddington et al., 2004; Song and Strassel, 2008) and ERE (Aguilar et al., 2014; Song et al., 2015) and their extensions for other programs such as DEFT [4], as well as publicly available resources such as YAGO (Suchanek et al., 2007; Hoffart et al., 2013; Mahdisoltani et al., 2015; Pellissier Tanon et al., 2020), FrameNet (Fillmore and Baker, 2009), PropBank (Kingsbury and Palmer, 2002), VerbNet (Kipper-Schuler, 2005) and the Reference Event Ontology (Brown et al., 2017).

An ongoing tension existed between performers' desires for expressive, expansive ontology models and LDC's need for a manageable ontology supporting cost-effective corpus construction and annotation that can assist in evaluation of resulting system output (Tracey et al., 2022). AIDA's solution was to charge LDC with selecting from previous programs those elements of the Program Ontology that would support salient entities and events in current program evaluation scenarios. This approach resulted in a patchwork AIDA Annotation Ontology where the connections between different ontological elements were sometimes obscured. For instance, Geographical Areas and Geographical Points were suggested in the Program Ontology, but without clear definitions. LDC chose Geographical Points to define a Location subtype that could be used for Addresses. They chose Geographical Areas to define a subtype of Facility that could be used for installations covering a significant area, larger than a point, such as Borders and Checkpoints. This choice of labels helped annotators to distinguish Addresses and Borders from other types of Locations and Facilities, but can be confusing to ontologists more familiar with Geographical Point and Area as two subtypes of Spatial Region.

The MAA and KAIROS programs described below both relied heavily on the AIDA Annotation Ontology, reflecting ongoing program needs for an expressive ontological data model that can be easily

[3]https://www.wikidata.org/

[4]https://www.darpa.mil/program/deep-exploration-and-filtering-of-text

extended to new domains and evaluation scenarios.

Modeling Adversarial Activity (MAA), now completed, was directed towards mathematical and computational methods for graph alignment and merging as well as subgraph detection and subgraph matching. MAA used the AIDA ontology, and MAA graphs were direct projections of AIDA RDF graphs into a property graph format that supported efficient and scalable graph analytics developed by MAA performers. MAA predominantly used the LDC Annotation Ontology as encoded in the AIDA Interchange Format. MAA also focused on the transactional aspects of interactions in addition to entity- and event-based knowledge graphs. The MAA evaluation phase included data sources related to financial topics, e.g. scientific publications and social media, and required modeling temporal events and entities with both physical and abstract attributes. In addition to the modeling of such data sources, the AIDA Annotation Ontology was also used by MAA performers to develop approximate entity alignment and subgraph matching algorithms.

Knowledge-directed Artificial Intelligence Reasoning Over Schemas (KAIROS) is ongoing and shifts the focus from the alternative hypotheses in AIDA to extracting sequences of events with temporal structure, such as narrative schemas. The goal is an AI system that can identify, link and temporally sequence complex events and their subsidiary elements and participants. For KAIROS the TA1's induce new schemas to create a library of schemas, and the TA2's are supposed to detect instances of these schemas in data. Since the schemas are intended to abstract away from the specific words and phrases that initially indicate them, there is a similar reliance on ontological types. A major focus of the first phase of KAIROS was the identification and definition of a set of Event Primitives that can comprise the schema elements. Most of these are recycled from AIDA, although sometimes at a more coarse-grained level. New ones have also been defined. During this effort, additional argument slots were added to many of the AIDA events.

The suggestion of shifting focus to Wikidata was made during the attempts to merge AIDA entity and event types into a nascent KAIROS ontology. Trying to quickly expand an existing although partial AIDA ontology to cover new domains highlighted its gaps as well as the difficulty of finding rational locations for new types without recourse to an overarching upper level ontology. Wikidata was not originally expected or intended to follow good principles of ontology development (Noy and Mcguinness, 2001), but a lot of effort on the part of many conscientious contributors had resulted in a reasonable approximation. After a few successful experiments with mapping the existing AIDA and KAIROS Entity and Event types to Wikdata Qnodes, a Cross-Program Ontology subcommittee was formed. DARPA approved the subcommittee's proposal to adopt Wikidata as a shared, general resource for entity and event identification, and the DARPA Wikidata Overlay was born.

The DWD Overlay should be contrasted with DARPA Wikidata (DWD), which is a large Wikidata dump adhering to the AIDA "Time Machine" constraint: due to the program's strict evaluation schedule, to properly track the inferences the systems are making automatically, it is sometimes necessary to ensure that program performers do not have access to vital information that they are supposed to detect or induce automatically. Thus, the DWD takes a large portion of Wikidata restricted to information before 2010. The DWD itself has enabled research on knowledge graphs (Wang et al., 2022). The overlay started by pulling only from DWD during the programs, but has expanded into the full Wikidata catalog.

3 Methodology

Node type	Total	Top level	PropBank
Entities	276	68	0
Events	5,167	479	5,164
Relations	216	152	144
Temporal relations	8	8	1

Table 1: Current coverage of the overlay, version 5.4.5.

The first task in the shift from the comparatively small, domain-specific LDC annotation tagset to Wikidata involved manually mapping the 200+ AIDA/KAIROS LDC Entity, Relation and Event types, subtypes and sub-subtypes to Wikidata Qnodes. Every such mapping was subject to at least two passes from human curators, sometimes with conflicts generating extensive discussion with a larger group. In cases of dispute between a Qnode and its superclass, the superclass was selected to ensure wider coverage. Existing Entities, Relations and Events were carefully examined in turn, and an upper-middle level ontology for each category was manually extracted from Wikidata, and subjected to careful vetting, to simplify down stream inference tasks.

Because Wikidata Qnodes are especially oriented towards entities rather than events, entities were relatively straightforward. Events are difficult to delineate and place in hierarchies, making their representation inconsistent across ontologies. Mapping AIDA/KAIROS events to Wikidata Qnodes was therefore unsurprisingly more difficult than mapping the entities. Several AIDA/KAIROS event types were found to have no plausible Wikidata Qnode. Mapping the AIDA/KAIROS relations to Wikidata also required careful manual effort. As many relations as possible were mapped to Pnodes. However, in cases where no Pnode could be found for an AIDA/KAIROS relation, it was mapped to a Qnode.

3.1 Enriching Wikidata events with PropBank roles

Step 1: a semi-automatic mapping. Because Wikidata provides no information about the participants or arguments of an event, we added this information semi-automatically to an expansion of the original 132 DWD events that were based on LDC event types. Around 5,000 additional Qnodes were identified as event classes (e.g., Q7944 "earthquake" – a class vs. Q211386 "1906 San Francisco Earthquake" – an instance) and linked to PropBank rolesets using rules. In Wikidata, class Qnodes have a "subclass of" property that points to one or more class Qnodes (e.g., Q7944 "earthquake" is a subclass of Q8065 "natural disaster"). A Qnode was considered an "event candidate" if it was a descendant (a direct or indirect subclass) of the Wikidata event Q1190554 "occurrence". This filtering produced close to 30,000 "event candidates" many of which we would not consider events. For example, in Wikidata, Q18534 "metaphor" is a descendant from "occurrence". We created an exclusion list of 11 high-level non-events such as Q223557 "physical object" and eliminated all event candidates that descended only from the Qnodes on the exclusion list. After some manual editing, we ended up with about 4,500 Qnode events.

Next, we used PropBank rolesets to create argument frames for the event Qnodes. We used lexical matching of the node and roleset labels and aliases to obtain a rough mapping of Qnodes to rolesets. When a Qnode did not lexically match any rolesets, we ascended the class hierarchy to find the nearest ancestor with a roleset mapping. This resulted in many events mapped to the same roleset, e.g., many specific diseases mapped to ill.01. While this produced reasonable argument frames for most of the event Qnodes, it was a noisy mapping from the PropBank rolesets to Qnodes with many rolesets mapped to multiple Qnodes. The number of Qnodes per roleset was somewhat reduced by excluding the subclasses of the mapped nodes, e.g., if roleset R was mapped to Q1 and Q2 and Q2 was a descendant of Q1, Q2 was deleted from the mapping. But that still left many one-to-many mappings and quite a few one-to-one mappings were not optimal.

Step 2: comprehensive annotation. Because these one-to-many mappings presented a problem for performers, a manual review was initiated for the PropBank-Wikidata mappings, starting with those PropBank rolesets that map to more than 10 Wikidata nodes. The review expanded into an ongoing comprehensive annotation project. Annotators evaluate the degree to which existing Wikidata Qnodes match each PropBank roleset (there are 11,277 rolesets total, the 5000 from above are being reviewed first). Existing Qnodes that closely match the general meaning and granularity of a PropBank roleset are preserved. In cases where no suitable Qnode can be found for a roleset, annotators recommend adding a new Qnode to Wikidata itself to match the sense of the roleset exactly. Additionally, when a Wikidata Qnode and a PropBank roleset are related but differ in scope, annotators document the cause of a mismatch for use in creating more fine-grained mapping relationships. Table 2 summarizes the progress of the mapping. Finally, annotators check for incorrect semi-automatic mappings, ensuring that only high quality mapping are retained.

Event templates. Finally, every event in the overlay is enriched with event templates based on their PropBank mapping, which provide a way to induce past-tense natural language sentences from extracted events with slots filled. For example, Q11398090 "creation" has this template:

```
<A0_pag_creator> created <A1_ppt_thing_
created> using <A2_vsp_materials_used>
at <AM_loc>
```

Just like with the PropBank roles, templates were first automatically generated and then a slower manual curation process was initiated to vet the templates and ensure quality. Some automatically generated templates are not grammatical but are still included for broader, albeit noisier, coverage. The templates can be used in encoder-decoder models for argument extraction (Li et al., 2021; Du et al., 2022) as well as for easier human browsing and analysis in both the overlay itself and after event extraction.

3.2 Enriching Wikidata relations with PropBank roles

LDC began with a small amount of relations geared towards specific domains, spanning topics such as affiliations, locations, personal relationships, measurements, and part-whole relations. The relations worked for the domains they were built for, but were not comprehensive enough for open domain text, and the hierarchical structure was geared more towards ease of annotation rather than robust, principled ontological representation.

Relations are represented in Wikidata as Pnodes (P for "property") which allow for relational <*subject, Pnode, object*> triples to act as the main expressive component (triples are called "statements") in Wikidata.

Manually mapping Pnodes to PropBank. Often, Pnodes lend themselves to mapping to PropBank roles (e.g. P50 *author* maps cleanly to two roles in the author.01 roleset in PropBank). To offer more support for relation extraction and inference using the overlay, we began mapping these relation Pnodes to PropBank rolesets, as well. Out of the 216 relations currently listed in the overlay, 144 have PropBank mappings. Other Pnodes do not map easily to PropBank; for example, P1120 "number of deaths" implies a more complex event causing multiple deaths that doesn't correspond to a single verb, and the roleset "die.01" doesn't necessarily imply multiple deaths and thus does not have a specific slot for quantity. Future work may include additional event decompositions of such Pnodes, taking causality into account, but is not included in the current version of the overlay.

3.3 Event-event relations

In addition to the mapping of the original LDC Relations and the additional Pnode relations, special attention was paid to temporal relations. The overlay identifies a handful of Wikidata Qnodes and Pnodes as temporal relations based on Allen's

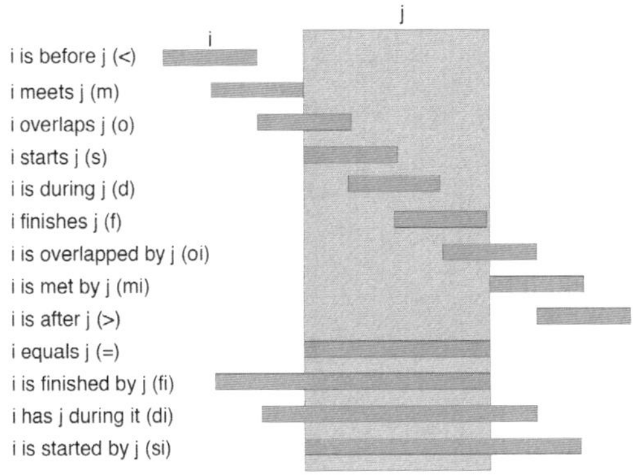

Figure 1: The full 13 relations from Allen's Interval Temporal Logic (Allen, 1983).

Interval Temporal Logic (Allen, 1983, 1984), exemplified in Figure 1.

Event reasoning requires temporal reasoning, which is concerned with representing and reasoning about both anchoring and ordering relationships between temporal intervals and events. Temporally situating events in a narrative involves two strategies: establishing a *relative ordering* of the events to each other, and a *temporal anchoring* of each event relative to a fixed time, such as an overt temporal expression, *yesterday*, or Reichenbach's speech time (Reichenbach, 1947). To this end, we adopt Allen's interval temporal logic (Allen, 1983, 1984), which is an attempt to model events directly in a temporal relation calculus. In this system, temporal intervals are considered primitives, while constraints (e.g., on actions) are expressed as relations between intervals. There are 13 basic (binary) interval relations, where six are inverses of the other, excluding equality.

Allen's interval-based notion of events also forms the interpretive core of TimeML (Pustejovsky et al., 2003), ISO-TimeML (Pustejovsky, 2017), the multilingual resources built on ISO-TimeML community (Im et al., 2009; Bittar et al., 2011; Caselli et al., 2011), as well as the shared tasks based on ISO-TimeML (Verhagen et al., 2007, 2010; UzZaman et al., 2012). The representation of events as reified intervals with constraints can be mapped to formal calculi used in temporal reasoning, e.g., DAML-Time (Hobbs and Pustejovsky, 2003), as well as Interval Temporal Logic (Pratt-Hartmann, 2007). This strategy also allows one to interpret the ordering of events in discourse and narratives as an interval constraint satisfaction problem, which has had a significant influence on recog-

	Semi-automatic	Human	Total mappings
Original (v5.3.0)	4,567	136	4,703
Mapping changed	*- 121*	*+ 121*	
Mapping retained	*- 406*	*+ 406*	*= 989 unique Qnodes*
Mapping added	*- 0*	*+ 462*	*covering 1,089 rolesets*
Current (v5.4.5)	4,040	1,125	5,165
New Qnodes recommended		2,792	

Table 2: A summary of the progress on PropBank-Wikidata annotation integration into the DWD overlay. *Italics* show human-curated PropBank-Qnode mappings: either retained from the original semi-automatic mapping, changed from the original, or added from outside the original 4.5k). The bottom row shows that around 2,800 rolesets were found the have no plausible Qnode by humans, and a Qnode addition to Wikidata was recommended.

nizing narrative event chains and identifying event schemas (Chambers and Jurafsky, 2008, 2009), as well as more recent work on script learning and frame induction (Cheung et al., 2013; Pichotta and Mooney, 2014).

Q/Pnode	Label	Allen interval
Q79030196	before	i is before j
P156	followed by	i meets j
P155	follows	i is met by j
P1382	partially coincident with	i and j partially overlap
Q6014822	inclusion	i occurs within j
Q79030284	after	i is after j
Q842346	equality	i equals j

Table 3: Wikidata nodes that represent temporal relations based on Allen intervals

4 Discussion

Use cases and limitations. The DWD overlay has mainly been used (Zhan et al., 2023) as the primary resource for general-purpose event extraction. The PropBank mappings in the overlay enabled Zhan et al. (2023) to create a large dataset starting from PropBank annotations and ending with Wikidata event Qnodes chosen from our mappings by Mechanical Turk workers.

Although the overlay has facilitated these advances in event extraction, many limitations have been identified. The many-to-one mappings (many Qnodes per PropBank roleset) proved to be the biggest limiting factor, as well as inaccuracy of automatic mappings, and the inclusion of low frequency nodes. The ongoing annotation project described in Section 3.1 should ameliorate these limitations.

Tension between resources. The same advantages we gain from combining Wikidata with PropBank—extensive coverage of real-world entities and concepts, plus a large, rich set of participant roles for events—create the largest problems. Both resources are powerful as NLP tools in their own right, each created for a slightly different purpose under a slightly different ethos. As discussed in Section 3, PropBank is action and event oriented, while Wikidata is oriented towards entities, more often containing nominalizations and nominal forms of events, if an event is represented at *all*.

When determining how entity-denoting nodes in Wikidata are to be mapped to PropBank event predicates, it is useful to examine how events are lexicalized in language. For English, the most frequent lexical realization of an event is a predicative verb, e.g., *eat*, *sink*, *write*, *sign*. This is followed by event nominalizations (e.g., *arrival*, *explosion*, *decay*) and activity nominalizations (e.g., *eating*, *sinking*, *writing*), and finally event nominals, e.g., *meal*, *war*, *accident*. As mentioned above, since Wikidata is largely organized around reified (entity-centric) conceptual nodes, it is not surprising that both nominalizations and nominal forms are more commonly represented as Qnodes for event denotations. For example, event predicates denoting activities that have clearly unambiguous nominalizations can be found represented as Qnodes in Wikidata:

- **Activity Nominalization**:
  eat.01 - eating_Q213449
  sink.01 - sinking_Q30880545
  write.01 - writing_Q86647781
  sign.01 - * "signing" is a specialized sense

In these cases, the PropBank mapping is easy. Many reifications of event nominalizations in Wikidata, however, tend to denote the result of the event, rather than the activity or event itself:

- **Result Nominalization**:

sign.01 - sign_Q3695082/signature_Q188675
dream.01 - dream_Q36348

Hence, mapping from Wikidata concepts to PropBank participant roles requires discernment between concepts that map to events themselves and concepts that should fill participant slots of events that are not represented in Wikidata at all.

Deciding when to allow imperfect mappings for the sake of coverage, yet at the expense of semantic integrity, has been a constant tension in the annotation project. For this reason, our annotators have recommended adding thousands of Qnodes to Wikidata itself to match the sense of PropBank rolesets exactly.

5 Future Work

The PropBank-Wikidata annotation project is still ongoing. The overlay is expected to become higher quality and less noisy as the project progresses. However, we hope to eventually *retire* the overlay by integrating it into Wikidata itself. Integrating our mappings into Wikidata itself will allow maintenance to be handled by the crowd-sourcers that already maintain Wikidata. In the meantime, we anticipate that our unique resource provides opportunities for further advancements in the field of semantic annotation and ontologies for natural language processing.

5.1 Adding event structures to Wikidata itself

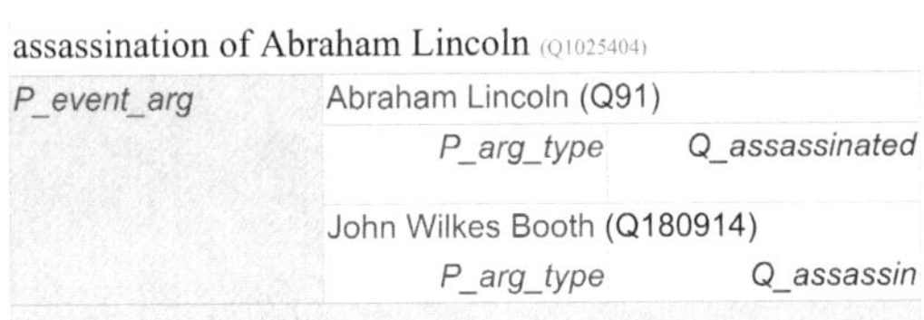

Figure 2: Sample of a Wikidata statement including proposed Pnodes and Qnodes for event arguments based on PropBank. Proposed nodes in *italics*.

We plan to incorporate our mapped PropBank roles into Wikidata itself. By moving these roles into Wikidata, researchers will eventually be able to use Wikidata directly and repeated updating of the DWD would not be necessary. In discussions with Wikidata, it was suggested we hire a Wikidata consultant—someone who is already a frequent contributor to Wikidata—to assist in adding information to Wikidata itself. It was also decided to first release this addition to Wikidata as an appendix. This would allow users to try the enhancement before fully altering the main Wikidata structure.

Specifically, we propose using new special-purpose Qnodes to represent event arguments in Wikidata. For example, the 'killer' in Q844482 (killing) will be Q_Q844482_killer (with the appropriate number replacing the '_Q844482_killer' part). These "event role" Qnodes will include the following proposed Pnodes: P_role_index, P_role_function, P_role_description, P_role_in, and P_selectional_preference, which are shown in Table 4 exemplifying their usage for the proposed *killer* Qnode.

Multiple statements with P_selectional _preference should be interpreted as an "OR", i.e., the filler of the role slot should descend from at least one of the selectional preference Qnodes. The meaning of "descend" could be application-specific, but, generally, we mean a combination of "subclass of", "parent taxon" and "instance of" properties.

Once we complete the mapping of the PropBank rolesets to Wikidata Qnodes, we can create the event role Qnodes automatically. Since there are about 11,400 PropBank rolesets with 2-4 roles each, we can expect about 25,000-40,000 new event role Qnodes. It might also be possible to cluster the event role Qnodes and create a "subclass of" hierarchy. We want to stress that the proposed event role Qnodes are not lexical or grammatical constructs. The existence of a killer in a killing event is not tied to any language or grammar. It is a part of the "killing" concept.

Wikidata contains many Qnodes representing event instances. For example, Q1025404 (assassination of Abraham Lincoln) is an instance of Q3882219 (assassination). Our proposal will create Q_assassin and Q_assassinated event role Qnodes. We propose to create one new property P_event_arg with a qualifier P_arg_type to represent the roles in an event instance, which we show in Figure 2.

In the process of mapping PropBank to Wikidata, we have identified hundreds of gaps in coverage in the Wikidata event hierarchy. Therefore, we additionally plan to add event Qnodes where our annotators noted they could find no matching Qnodes for a particular PropBank roleset.

5.2 Evaluation of ontologies

Ontologies can be *formally* evaluated via principles (Oltramari et al., 2010). These modes of evalu-

Proposed Pnode	Possible values	Value for Q_killer
role index	0, 1, 2, ... or "M"	0
role function	a Qnode representing PropBank role functions	Q392648 (agent)
role description	a string	"killer"
role in	the event class Qnode	Q844482 (killing)
selectional preference	a Qnode which stipulates the ancestor of the potential role filler	Q5 (human)

Table 4: Our proposed Pnode additions to Wikidata that give information for the event arguments of event role Qnodes.

ation are time- and resource-consuming, requiring philosophical training and manual human effort. Another mode of evaluating ontologies is application-based: one can rank ontologies based on metrics used for applications of the ontologies themselves. From this observation, a few different research questions that we could answer with our overlay emerge: do ontologies that receive a positive formal evaluation also perform well on NLP tasks? Has our manual curation work resulted in better downstream performance, or a better evaluation using formal principles? We would like to address these questions in future work, along with exploring different ways of incorporating this resource into downstream applications.

6 Conclusion

We introduced the DWD Overlay, a curated subset of Wikidata enriched with PropBank roles for use as an ontology for natural language processing. Our mapping combines the extensive coverage of ontological concepts and the inference power of Wikidata with participant roles in PropBank, providing a comprehensive, open domain resource for information extraction especially geared toward natural language newstext. While the DWD Overlay already includes 1,125 manually curated Qnode-PropBank mappings and 4,040 semi-automatically induced Qnode-PropBank mappings, event templates for every event, as well as mappings to Allen Interval Temporal Logic relations, the human annotation is still a work in progress and the overlay is expected to continue to increase in quality.

Acknowledgments

We gratefully acknowledge the support of DARPA FA8750-18-2-0016-AIDA – RAMFIS: Representations of vectors and Abstract Meanings for Information Synthesis and a sub award from RPI on DARPA KAIROS Program No. FA8750-19-2-1004. Any opinions, findings, and conclusions or recommendations expressed in this material are those of the authors and do not necessarily reflect the views of DARPA or the U.S. government.

References

Jacqueline Aguilar, Charley Beller, Paul McNamee, Benjamin Van Durme, Stephanie Strassel, Zhiyi Song, and Joe Ellis. 2014. A comparison of the events and relations across ACE, ERE, TAC-KBP, and FrameNet annotation standards. In *Proceedings of the Second Workshop on EVENTS: Definition, Detection, Coreference, and Representation*, pages 45–53, Baltimore, Maryland, USA. Association for Computational Linguistics.

James F. Allen. 1983. Maintaining knowledge about temporal intervals. *Communications of the ACM*, 26(11):832–843.

James F Allen. 1984. Towards a general theory of action and time. *Artificial intelligence*, 23(2):123–154.

André Bittar, Pascal Amsili, Pascal Denis, and Laurence Danlos. 2011. French timebank: an iso-timeml annotated reference corpus. In *Proceedings of the 49th Annual Meeting of the Association for Computational Linguistics: Human Language Technologies: short papers-Volume 2*, pages 130–134. Association for Computational Linguistics.

Susan Windisch Brown, Claire Bonial, Leo Obrst, and Martha Palmer. 2017. The rich event ontology. In *Proceedings of the Events and Stories in the News Workshop*, pages 87–97.

Aljoscha Burchardt, Katrin Erk, Anette Frank, Andrea Kowalski, Sebastian Pado, and Manfred Pinkal. 2006. The salsa corpus: a german corpus resource for lexical semantics. In *Proceedings of LREC*, Genoa, Italy.

Tommaso Caselli, Valentina Bartalesi Lenzi, Rachele Sprugnoli, Emanuele Pianta, and Irina Prodanof. 2011. Annotating events, temporal expressions and relations in Italian: the It-TimeML experience for the Ita-TimeBank. In *Proceedings of the 5th Linguistic Annotation Workshop*, pages 143–151. Association for Computational Linguistics.

Nathanael Chambers and Dan Jurafsky. 2008. Jointly combining implicit constraints improves temporal ordering. In *Proceedings of the Conference on Empiri-*

cal Methods in Natural Language Processing, pages 698–706. Association for Computational Linguistics.

Nathanael Chambers and Dan Jurafsky. 2009. Unsupervised learning of narrative schemas and their participants. In *Proceedings of the Joint Conference of the 47th Annual Meeting of the ACL and the 4th International Joint Conference on Natural Language Processing of the AFNLP: Volume 2-Volume 2*, pages 602–610. Association for Computational Linguistics.

Jackie Chi Kit Cheung, Hoifung Poon, and Lucy Vanderwende. 2013. Probabilistic frame induction. *arXiv preprint arXiv:1302.4813*.

George Doddington, Alexis Mitchell, Mark Przybocki, Lance Ramshaw, Stephanie Strassel, and Ralph Weischedel. 2004. The automatic content extraction (ACE) program – tasks, data, and evaluation. In *Proceedings of the Fourth International Conference on Language Resources and Evaluation (LREC'04)*, Lisbon, Portugal. European Language Resources Association (ELRA).

Xinya Du, Zixuan Zhang, Sha Li, Pengfei Yu, Hongwei Wang, Tuan Lai, Xudong Lin, Ziqi Wang, Iris Liu, Ben Zhou, Haoyang Wen, Manling Li, Darryl Hannan, Jie Lei, Hyounghun Kim, Rotem Dror, Haoyu Wang, Michael Regan, Qi Zeng, Qing Lyu, Charles Yu, Carl Edwards, Xiaomeng Jin, Yizhu Jiao, Ghazaleh Kazeminejad, Zhenhailong Wang, Chris Callison-Burch, Mohit Bansal, Carl Vondrick, Jiawei Han, Dan Roth, Shih-Fu Chang, Martha Palmer, and Heng Ji. 2022. RESIN-11: Schema-guided event prediction for 11 newsworthy scenarios. In *Proceedings of the 2022 Conference of the North American Chapter of the Association for Computational Linguistics: Human Language Technologies: System Demonstrations*, pages 54–63, Hybrid: Seattle, Washington + Online. Association for Computational Linguistics.

Charles J. Fillmore and Collin Baker. 2009. 313 A Frames Approach to Semantic Analysis. In *The Oxford Handbook of Linguistic Analysis*. Oxford University Press.

Jerry Hobbs and James Pustejovsky. 2003. Annotating and reasoning about time and events. In *Proceedings of AAAI Spring Symposium on Logical Formalizations of Commonsense Reasoning*, volume 3.

Johannes Hoffart, Fabian M. Suchanek, Klaus Berberich, and Gerhard Weikum. 2013. YAGO2: A spatially and temporally enhanced knowledge base from wikipedia. *Artificial Intelligence*, 194:28–61.

Seohyun Im, Hyunjo You, Hayun Jang, Seungho Nam, and Hyopil Shin. 2009. Ktimeml: specification of temporal and event expressions in korean text. In *Proceedings of the 7th Workshop on Asian Language Resources*, pages 115–122. Association for Computational Linguistics.

Paul R Kingsbury and Martha Palmer. 2002. From TreeBank to PropBank. In *LREC*, pages 1989–1993.

Karin Kipper-Schuler. 2005. *VerbNet: A broad-coverage, comprehensive verb lexicon*. Ph.D. thesis, University of Pennsylvania.

Sha Li, Heng Ji, and Jiawei Han. 2021. Document-level event argument extraction by conditional generation. In *Proceedings of the 2021 Conference of the North American Chapter of the Association for Computational Linguistics: Human Language Technologies*, pages 894–908, Online. Association for Computational Linguistics.

Farzaneh Mahdisoltani, Joanna Asia Biega, and Fabian M. Suchanek. 2015. YAGO3: A knowledge base from multilingual Wikipedias. In *Conference on Innovative Data Systems Research*.

N. Noy and Deborah Mcguinness. 2001. Ontology development 101: A guide to creating your first ontology. *Knowledge Systems Laboratory*, 32.

Alessandro Oltramari, Aldo Gangemi, Chu-Ren Huang, Nicoletta Calzolari, Alessandro Lenci, and Laurent Prévot. 2010. *Synergizing ontologies and the lexicon: a roadmap*, 1 edition, page 72–78. Cambridge University Press.

Thomas Pellissier Tanon, Gerhard Weikum, and Fabian Suchanek. 2020. YAGO 4: A reason-able knowledge base. In *The Semantic Web*, page 583–596, Cham. Springer International Publishing.

Karl Pichotta and Raymond Mooney. 2014. Statistical script learning with multi-argument events. In *Proceedings of the 14th Conference of the European Chapter of the Association for Computational Linguistics*, pages 220–229.

I Pratt-Hartmann. 2007. From timeml to interval temporal logic. In *Proceedings of the Seventh International Workshop on Computational Semantics (IWCS-7)*, pages 166–180.

James Pustejovsky. 2017. Iso-timeml and the annotation of temporal information. In *Handbook of Linguistic Annotation*, pages 941–968. Springer.

James Pustejovsky, José M Castano, Robert Ingria, Roser Sauri, Robert J Gaizauskas, Andrea Setzer, Graham Katz, and Dragomir R Radev. 2003. Timeml: Robust specification of event and temporal expressions in text. *New directions in question answering*, 3:28–34.

Hans Reichenbach. 1947. *Elements of Symbolic Logic*. The Free Press; London: Collier-Macmillan.

Zhiyi Song, Ann Bies, Stephanie Strassel, Tom Riese, Justin Mott, Joe Ellis, Jonathan Wright, Seth Kulick, Neville Ryant, and Xiaoyi Ma. 2015. From light to rich ERE: Annotation of entities, relations, and events. In *Proceedings of the The 3rd Workshop on EVENTS: Definition, Detection, Coreference, and Representation*, pages 89–98, Denver, Colorado. Association for Computational Linguistics.

Zhiyi Song and Stephanie Strassel. 2008. Entity translation and alignment in the ACE-07 ET task. In *Proceedings of the Sixth International Conference on Language Resources and Evaluation (LREC'08)*, Marrakech, Morocco. European Language Resources Association (ELRA).

Stephanie Strassel and Alexis Mitchell. 2003. Multilingual resources for entity extraction. In *Proceedings of the ACL 2003 Workshop on Multilingual and Mixed-language Named Entity Recognition*, pages 49–56, Sapporo, Japan. Association for Computational Linguistics.

Fabian M. Suchanek, Gjergji Kasneci, and Gerhard Weikum. 2007. Yago: A core of semantic knowledge. In *Proceedings of the 16th International Conference on World Wide Web*, WWW '07, page 697–706, New York, NY, USA. Association for Computing Machinery.

Jennifer Tracey, Ann Bies, Jeremy Getman, Kira Griffitt, and Stephanie Strassel. 2022. A study in contradiction: Data and annotation for aida focusing on informational conflict in russia-ukraine relations. In *Proceedings of the Thirteenth Language Resources and Evaluation Conference*, pages 1831–1838.

Naushad UzZaman, Hector Llorens, James Allen, Leon Derczynski, Marc Verhagen, and James Pustejovsky. 2012. Tempeval-3: Evaluating events, time expressions, and temporal relations. *arXiv preprint arXiv:1206.5333*.

Marc Verhagen, Robert Gaizauskas, Frank Schilder, Mark Hepple, Graham Katz, and James Pustejovsky. 2007. Semeval-2007 task 15: Tempeval temporal relation identification. In *Proceedings of the fourth international workshop on semantic evaluations (SemEval-2007)*, pages 75–80.

Marc Verhagen, Roser Sauri, Tommaso Caselli, and James Pustejovsky. 2010. Semeval-2010 task 13: Tempeval-2. In *Proceedings of the 5th international workshop on semantic evaluation*, pages 57–62.

Denny Vrandečić and Markus Krötzsch. 2014. Wikidata: a free collaborative knowledgebase. *Communications of the ACM*, 57(10):78–85.

Jiang Wang, Filip Ilievski, Pedro Szekely, and Ke-Thia Yao. 2022. Augmenting knowledge graphs for better link prediction. In *Proceedings of the Thirty-First International Joint Conference on Artificial Intelligence*, page 2277–2283, Vienna, Austria. International Joint Conferences on Artificial Intelligence Organization.

Qiusi Zhan, Sha Li, Kathryn Conger, Martha Palmer, Heng Ji, and Jiawei Han. 2023. GLEN: General-purpose event detection for thousands of types. Preprint on webpage at `https://arxiv.org/abs/2303.09093`.

Semantic Annotation of Verbs of Contact in Bulgarian

Maria A. Todorova
Institute for Bulgarian Language, Bulgarian Academy of Sciences
maria@dcl.bas.bg

Abstract

The paper presents the work on the selection, semantic annotation and classification of a group of verbs of contact as defined in the Bulgarian WordNet (i.e. verbs assigned the semantic primitive 'verb.contact') which belong to the general lexis of Bulgarian. I describe in brief the selection of the verbs to be analyzed according to two different criteria: (i) statistical information from corpora; (ii) membership of the verbs to the WordNet Base Concept set and information about their age of acquisition (AoA). The focus of the work is on the process of semantic annotation of the verbs, using combined information from two language resources – WordNet and FrameNet. The verbs of contact extracted from WordNet are assigned semantic frames from FrameNet and then grouped into semantic subclasses on the basis of their place in the WordNet hierarchy and the semantic restrictions imposed on the frame elements denoting the verbs' principal participants along with their syntactic realization. I offer some conclusions on the classification of 'verbs of contact' into semantic subtypes.

1 Introduction

Verb classes are sets of verbs sharing similar semantic properties, such as the membership to a common semantic domain or similar argument realization and semantic interpretation. Fillmore (1970) emphasizes the importance of verb classes in various tasks including the study of the patterns of shared verb behavior; the organization of the verb lexicon; the identification of grammatically relevant elements of meaning.

WordNet and FrameNet are large lexical resources that provide semantic information about verb classes. WordNet (WN) (Fellbaum, 1999) represents a multilingual conceptual network of synonym sets (synsets) linked by means of semantic relations such as hypernymy, antonymy, etc. FrameNet (FN) (Baker et al., 1998) represents the semantics of lexemes by means of schematic representations (frames) describing objects, situations, or events and their components (frame elements) in the apparatus of Frame Semantics.

The aim of this paper is to present an ongoing work on the semantic annotation and classification of a subset of Bulgarian 'verbs of contact' that belong to the general lexis of Bulgarian. The goal of these efforts is to contribute both to the enrichment of the Bulgarian WordNet with Conceptual frames (Koeva, 2020) and to the enlargement of the Bulgarian FrameNet, and hence – to the creation of a linked semantic and syntactic resource.

Verbs of Contact In general, the notion of CONTACT is understood as a "conceptual core element" of a predicate (Juffs, 1996). The set of verbs of contact in WordNet features the ones included in the relevant lexicographer's file, one of 15 files in which the verbs in WordNet are grouped according to the semantic domain to which they pertain, and is defined as "verbs of touching, hitting, tying, digging" (Miller et al., 1990). It is also the largest of them, consisting of more than 820 synsets including event and action verbs that share the semantic component of CONTACT or IMPACT. This type of verb set cast taxonomic framework by means of the hyponymy (troponymy) relation, which covers a number of different manner relations (Fellbaum, 1990). The semantic definition of the class is fuzzy and does not really summarize the semantics of all the verbs it contains.

The remainder of the paper is organized as follows. Section 2 describes the data used in the process of annotation – a set of verbs of contact from WordNet and a set of semanic frames from FrameNet. Section 3 presents a revision of the related descriptions and classifications of the verbs under consideration. Section 4 discusses the semantic features of

Proceedings of the 19th Joint ACL - ISO Workshop on Interoperable Semantic Annotation, pages 11–17
June 20, 2023.

verbs of contact and their lexical semantic subtypes. Sections 5 and 6 offer details on the process of annotation of verbs of contact with semantic frames, while Sections 8 and 9 sum up the observations on the results and suggest directions for future work.

2 The data analyzed

The analyzed verbs and the corresponding semantic descriptions were extracted from the interrelated language resources: WordNet (Fellbaum, 1999) and FrameNet (Ruppenhofer et al., 2016). The combined information available in the resources results in a rich representation of the paradigmatic and syntagmatic aspects of lexical semantics (Baker and Fellbaum, 2009). The implementation of the mapping of FN frames to WN synsets is described in detail in Stoyanova and Leseva (2020). The selected set of verbs (i.e. the WN verbs of contact) was subsequently filtered so as to include only verbs belonging to the general lexis of Bulgarian.

Selection of General Lexis Verbs in Bulgarian The general verb lexis of Bulgarian was selected for the purposes of the theoretical semantic description and typology of verb predicates belonging to the basic conceptual apparatus of the language under consideration (Stoyanova and Leseva, 2020; Todorova et al., 2022). The collection was excerpted from a set of 44,000 English verbs selected according to the AoA (age of acquisition) criterion (Brysbaert and Biemiller, 2017) and a subset of verbs derived from the Bulgarian WordNet (BulNet) (Koeva, 2010), a lexical-semantic network for Bulgarian modeled on the Princeton WordNet (Miller et al., 1990; Miller, 1995). The 44,000 English verbs are related to the synonym sets that contain the corresponding verbs in BulNet. The verbs are also assigned: (i) a relevant label in case the corresponding synsets belong to the list of the so-called base concepts, or BCS[1], a subset of concepts that reflect the basic conceptual stock across languages; (ii) frequency information on the use of the verbs derived from the Bulgarian National Corpus (Koeva et al., 2012). The verbs are additionally evaluated by linguists, who, according to the available information from various resources and their intuition as native speakers, determine whether a concept expressed by a synonym set is part of the general lexis of Bulgarian and which of the literals (members of a synset) are the main representatives of the relevant sense[2]. This procedure resulted in a list of 2,027 general-lexis verbs, 381 of which belong to 133 synsets assigned the prime *verb.contact*. These 381 verbs constitute the starting set selected for annotation with semantic frames, that is being carried out at the moment. The main goal of the analysis is to propose a classification of the verbs of contact in Bulgarian on the basis of the description of their frame elements, their selectional restrictions (represented in terms of semantic classes of nouns) and syntactic expression.

3 Related Work

Verbs of contact are heterogeneous and overlapping as a semantic class and thus less studied than other verb classes. They have been an object of research for English Fillmore (1970); Levin (1993); Fellbaum (1990) and Chinese (Gao and Cheng, 2003). Fillmore (1970) focuses on two large classes of verbs of contact, *break* and *hit*, whose members share elements of meaning and patterns of behavior. A class of contact verbs was also defined by Levin (1993) in her semantic classification on the basis of a number of alternations reflecting the correlation between the semantics and the syntactic behavior of the verbs and the interpretation of their arguments. In particular, Levin (1993): (148-156) defines a class of *Verbs of contact by impact* with a number of subclasses: *Hit verbs; Spank verbs; Swat verbs; Non-agentive verbs*. Dimitrova-Vulchanova and Dekova (2009) represent a corpus and an empirically-derived classification of *verbs of contact by impact* using the Sign model formalism. Individual subtypes of the class were also described by some authors: *physical contact verb* (Gao, 2001) and *Hit and Spank verbs of contact by impact* from Gao and Cheng (2003). These descriptions and classifications partially overlap with the classification adopted in WordNet; their correspondences in FrameNet are less hierarchically structured. Previous work on the conceptual semantic annotation of Bulgarian verbs involves the analysis of verbs of change (Stoyanova and Leseva, 2021) and verbs of communication (Kukova, 2020). Different stages of the study of semantic

[1]The set of base concept synsets has been defined by the teams participating in the EuroWordNet and the BalkaNet projects http://globalwordnet.org/resources/gwa-base-concepts/

[2]The selection and evaluation of the verbs that form the set of general lexis of Bulgarian has been performed by the team of linguists at the Department of Computational Linguistics of the Institute for Bulgarian Language at the Bulgarian Academy of Sciences.

features and selectional restrictions relevant to the semantic description of Bulgarian verbs and their frame elements are explored in (Leseva et al., 2020, 2021). Verbs of contact have not been described for Bulgarian so far.

4 Semantic Features of Verbs of Contact

In this Section I use the semantic characterization of verbs of contact and their division into subclasses proposed by Fellbaum (1990) with a view to the WordNet hierarchy, in combination with additional semantic information from FrameNet.

Lexical Semantic Subtypes Being the largest class of verbs in WordNet, the set of contact verbs is well-represented in the selection of Bulgarian general lexis verbs – nearly 7% of the whole set. Most of the contact verbs are hypernyms of the following central verb concepts: *fasten, attach, cover, cut* and *touch*, which results in a large tree structure within the set (Fellbaum, 1990). Based on the WordNet hypernym relation, the following subgroups of contact verbs have been defined:
(a) Verbs encoding force, intensity, or iteration of the action (*hit*).
(b) Verbs of holding (*grab, squeeze, pinch*) and touching (*paw, finger, stroke, poke*).
(c) Verbs involving an instrument or material argument (*paint*).
(d) Verbs involving a body part argument indicating what kind of contact action the body part is typically used for: shoulder (*support, carry*); elbow (*push*); finger, thumb (*touch, manipulate*).

5 Annotation of Verbs of Contact and Semantic Frames Assignment

The annotation of Bulgarian contact verbs with semantic frames and the description of their semantic features – i.e. their frame elements[3] and the relevant semantic restrictions is part of the description of Conceptual frames in Bulgarian. Conceptual frames are abstract structures, that describe a particular types of situations or events, along with its participants and properties Koeva (2020). The annotation is carried out by means of a software system called BulFrame specifically designed for the definition and description of conceptual frames (Koeva and Doychev, 2022) The semantic restrictions imposed on the verb's arguments were aligned with (a) particular subtree(s) of noun synsets in WordNet and draw on previous efforts described in Leseva et al. (2018). The annotation of the selected verbs includes the following steps:
(a) Each verb is assigned a FrameNet frame (as is), a FrameNet frame that has been modified to better reflect the semantics of the verbs under discussion or a newly formulated frame.
(b) The restrictions which are relevant for the entire frame are examined and revised if needed; these restrictions have been defined on the basis of the combined semantic information from WN and FN.
(c) For each core frame element in a given frame a linguist checks the validity of the general selectional restrictions assigned to it. At this stage the linguist is able to verify the accuracy of the frame-to-synset assignment and to make changes if necessary. The restrictions assigned to a frame give a first approximation of the semantic specification of the frame elements. When a general restriction is assigned, all hyponyms of the noun synsets, representing the roots of the relevant subtrees [4], are potential candidates for the FE in context.
(d) Each verb is examined individually in order to specify additional selectional restrictions from WordNet if needed. Specific restrictions on the lexical realization of the FEs are represented as individual WN synsets.

6 Annotation of Verbs of Contact – Semantic Classes, Semantic Frames and Restrictions

In this Section I provide an analysis of the verbs of contact which have been assigned one of a number of selected frames denoting contact and a description of their selectional restrictions. The semantic restrictions describing the compatibility between semantic classes of verbs and nouns corresponding to their arguments proposed in Leseva et al. (2019) are aligned with the noun synsets representing the roots of the subtrees.
The grouping of *verbs of contact* into subtypes is based on the hypothesis that verbs with similar meanings have characteristic argument realization patterns shared by their members. It is necessary to take into account the semantics of a verb's arguments in order to determine whether a particular verb construction is acceptable. 31 frames were

[3]elements which correspond to core FEs in FrameNet are semantically essential components of a frame that can be recovered from the context

[4]A root is a node in the WordNet structure represented by a synset whose meaning constitutes a category under which more specific senses are subsumed

assigned to verbs of contact included in the selection of Bulgarian general lexis verbs so far. The contact predicates are divided into 2 subgroups that combine semantic components of *Contact via Motion* and *State Verbs for Physical Contact*. The most typical arguments in their semantic frames are Theme, Force, Body Part, Source, Frequency, and Instrument. Some of the frames are analyzed and commented below with a view to the assignment of more refined selectional restrictions.

6.1 Verbs of Physical Contact via Motion

This group includes the verbs assigned the following FN frames: *Becoming attached, Body movement, Breaking off, Cause fluidic motion, Closure, Destroying, Detaching, Dispersal, Filling, Fluidic motion, Food gathering, Gathering up, Grinding, Make noise, Manipulate into shape, Placing, Removing, Reshaping, Undressing, Processing materials.*

Verbs of contact denoting attaching, detaching, placing, removing, filling and emptying share common frame elements and restrictions. As a whole, these frames involve the movement of an entity (the Theme) either directed to (Goal) or originating from (Source) to a particular place. Their core frame elements share similar general restrictions – their Agents are volitional; the Cause denotes a physical entity or eventuality; the FE Item is a physical object, the Goal – a physical entity or container and the Connector – a physical entity. The semantics of the point of physical contact defines two main subgroups:

- verbs of contact on or along a surface (as the verb root *triya:2* [5] *(rub:2 eng-30-01249724-v) 'move over something with pressure'* and its hyponyms – *brush:7; gauge:6; scrub:3; smear:4; scrape:1*, etc.
- verbs of contact with a container (as the verb roots *palnya:1 (load:3 eng-30-01490336-v), izprazvam:8 (empty:7 eng-30-01488313-v)* and their hyponyms

As shown in Example 1 below many verbs impose narrower selectional restrictions that elaborate on the more general ones assigned to the frame[6].

[5]The Bulgarian examples transliterated in Latin script are followed by their correspondences in the Princeton WordNet

[6]The BulNet aligned with the English WordNet and other languages is available online on http://dcl.bas.bg/bulnet/

Example 1:
(a) the verb *tovarya:1 (load:2 eng-30-01489989-v) 'fill or place a load on'* is assigned the FN frame **Filling** which relates to *" ... filling Containers and covering areas with some thing(s) or substance – the Theme. The area or container can appear as the direct object with all these verbs, and is ... the goal of motion of the Theme".*[7] The analysis of the usage examples available for the verb show that the general selectional restrictions specified for the frame Filling are sufficient for the semantic description of the synset under consideration. In particular, the selectional restrictions for the Agent correspond to the WN root synset *person:1 (eng-30-00007846-n)*; the ones defined for the FE Theme correspond to the WN root synset *physical object: 1 (eng-30-00002684-n)* or *entity: 1 (eng-30-00001740-n)* and those specified for the Goal match the synset *container:1 (eng-30-03094503-n)*
(b) the verb *lakiram:1 (varnish:1 eng-30-01269008-v) 'cover with varnish'* imposes more specific restrictions to its core FEs. The Agent is a volitional human being, a qualified person, while the Theme is a particular kind of substance best described by means of the synset *lak:1 (varnish: 2 eng-30-04521987-n)* and the Goal is a *physical object:1 (eng-30-00002684-n)* or a *surface:1 (eng-30-08660339-n).*
In addition, in many cases, part of the synsets sharing the same FrameNet frame belong to the same (or to a semantically close) WordNet subtrees. In these cases the topmost synset more or less complies with the restrictions for the frame, whereas its hyponyms may impose more specific requirements (see Example 2 below).

Verbs of Bodily Contact include the verbs assigned the FrameNet frame **Manipulation** which describes *" ... the manipulation of an Entity by an Agent. Generally, this implies that the Entity is not deeply or permanently physically affected, nor is it overall moved from one place to another".* Example 2 illustrates the more specific restrictions specified for the core FEs of verb synsets assigned the frame Manipulation which are hyponyms of the synset hvashtham:7.
Example 2:
hvashtam:7 (hold:13 eng-30-01216670-v 'have or hold in one's hands or grip')
(a) hyponym: *stiskam:2 (grasp:3 'hold firmly')*

[7]https://framenet.icsi.berkeley.edu/

(b) hyponym: *pritiskam se:1 (clutch:4 'hold firmly, usually with one's hands')*
(c) hyponym: *lyuleya:3 (cradle:2 'hold gently and carefully')*
(d) hyponym: *sklyuchvam:6 (interlace:2 'hold in a locking position')*
(e) hyponym: *ulavyam (trap:4 'hold or catch as if in a trap')*
The restrictions on the FE Agent of the root verb and a part of its hyponyms differ: for some verbs the Agent is a volitional human being corresponding to the WN root synset person:1 (eng-30-00007846-n), e.g. (2b), (2d), while in other cases the verbs may allow their Agent to be an animal (2a), (2b), corresponding to the WN root synset animal: 1 (eng-30-08660339-n) or FE Body part, corresponding to (body part:1 eng-30-03183080-n), as in (2e).
The restrictions on the FE Entity also are not consistent in all the discussed members of the tree – Entity may be either an animate (2g) or an inanimate physical object (2d).

Verbs of Contact by Impact include the verbs assigned the FrameNet frames **Impact** defined as: *"While in motion, an Impactor makes sudden, forcible contact with the Impactee, or two Impactors both move, mutually making forcible contact"* as well as **Destroying**: *A Destroyer (a conscious entity) or Cause (an event, or an entity involved in such an event) affects the Patient negatively so that the Patient no longer exists.* Their core FEs share similar general semantic characteristics, so no more specific selectional restrictions can be defined – the Impactor and the Impactee may be physical entities or eventualities, devices or persons, as shown in Example 3. It illustrates verbs belonging to the WN subtree stemming from udryam:6 (hit:13), eng-30-01236164-v 'hit against; come into sudden contact with' which are assigned the FN frame *Impact*.
Example 3:
udryam:6 (smash:9 eng-30-00126236-n 'collide or strike violently and suddenly')
(a) hyponym: *sblaskvam (shock:6 'collide violently')*
(b) hyponym: *razbivam se: 2 (crash:6 'undergo damage or destruction on impact')*
The verbs in this example impose less rigid restrictions on their FEs – the Impactor and the Impactee correspond to physical entities.

6.2 State Verbs of Physical Contact

This group includes the verbs assigned the following FN frames: *Being wet, Distributed position, Posture, Spatial contact, Surrendering possession, Surrounding, Scouring*. These frames describe an Agent (Protagonist), Item, Theme, Figure or another entity's being on, in or in contact with an area or a substance (Location).
Example 4 shows verbs from the WN subtree stemming from *lezha:3 (lie:2* which are assigned the FN frame **Posture**: *An Agent supports their body in a particular Location. The LUs of the frame convey which body part is the Point of contact where the Agent is supported, what orientation the body is in, and some overall arrangement of the limbs (especially the legs) and the torso.*
Example 4:
lezha:3 (lie:2, eng-30-01547001-v 'be lying, be prostrate; be in a horizontal position') (a) hyponym: *peka se :1 (sunbathe:1 'expose one's body to the sun')*
(b) hyponym: *iztyagam se:1 (sprawl:1 'sit or lie with one's limbs spread out')*
(c) hyponym: *izlyagam se:1 (recumb:1 'lean in a comfortable resting position')*
(d) hyponym: *pokrivam:1 (overlie:2 'lie upon; lie on top of')*
(e) hyponym: *lezha buden:1 (lie awake:1 'lie without sleeping')*
(f) hyponym: *pochivam:3 (repose:6 'lie when dead')*
(g) hyponym: *pripicham se:1 (bask:1 'be exposed')*
The verbs belonging to the subtree under consideration impose more specific selectional restrictions on their Agent: for some of them it may be a volitional human being corresponding to the WN root synset person:1 (eng-30-00007846-n) (4e), (4f) as well as an animal (4a), (4b), (4c), (4d), (4g), aligned with the WN root synset animal:1 (eng-30-08660339-n). The FE Location is an adjunct in Bulgarian and can be omitted, and is thus not discussed here.

7 Syntactic Patterns

The observations on the syntactic behavior of the studied verbs led to the delineation of several general syntactic constructions within the group:
(a) *NP(pro-drop subject) Verb NP(direct object – Theme) PP(non-obligatory indirect object –*

to/on/over Destination) This syntactic structure is typical for verbs selecting a Theme as an object, for instance *razleya (pour) – Razlya chaya po masata. ('She poured the tea over the table').*
(b)*NP(pro-drop subject) Verb NP(direct object – Destination) PP(non-obligatory indirect object – with Theme).* This pattern is found with verbs taking the FE Destination as an object, for instance *namazha (spread) – Namaza filiyata s maslo. ('She spread butter on the slice').*
(c) *NP(pro-drop subject) Verb NP(direct object – Location/Container) PP(non-obligatory indirect object – with Theme).* This type of structure is typical for verbs selecting the FE Location/Container as an object as in *natovarya (load) – Natovariha kamiona s kutiite ('They loaded the truck with the boxes').*

8 Results and Discussion

The annotation results presented in the paper are preliminary as they are part of a work in progress. A total of 381 contact verbs were assigned 26 FN frames, most of which have been manually checked and assigned general selectional restrictions. The description of the syntactic properties and the definition of more specific selectional restrictions for each verb are still in process, covering mainly the root synsets (Section 6).
The contact verbs were grouped in two main subcategories – Verbs of Physical Contact via Motion and State Verbs of Physical Contact with different subgroups according to the features *manner* and *point of the contact.*
The process of annotation raises some interesting questions regarding the language-specific lexicalization patterns of some Bulgarian verbs as compared with their English counterparts. The syntactic expression of some of the FEs differs in the two languages. The obligatoriness of the syntactic realization depends on the point of contact between the core frame elements. The English verbs of contact that encode one of the frame elements in their morphological structure – e.g. the instrument (knife), the resultant shape (slice), the covering material (paint), the container (box, bag), etc. – have different lexicalization in Bulgarian. Not all the Bulgarian correspondences have the frame element incorporated in their word structure. For example the English verb *cream: 3 (eng-30-01364483-v 'put on cream, as on one's face or body')* – has no one-word correspondence in Bulgarian and is translated as the expression *namazvam s krem: 1,* where *krem* is the Theme, compare: *She creamed her face (Destination)* and *Namaza s krem (Theme) liceto si (Destination).*
On the other hand some of the Bulgaraian verb hyponyms express a specific manner by means of prefixation, e.g. *razryzvam: 2 (cut: 35 eng-30-01552519-v 'cut into pieces').* Such predicates lexicalize a meaning component which specifies a scale of motion or state and contact and do not have full one-word correspondences in English. These and other similar cases have necessitated the modification of FN frames or the definition of further specifications.
The above observations led to the hypothesis that different word formation mechanisms across the languages, such as derivation, compounding and conversion as well as lexical gaps, reflect differences in the semantic structure of lexemes.

9 Conclusions and Future Work

The research described in this paper is part of an effort towards the enrichment of the set of Bulgarian general lexis verbs derived from the Bulgarian WordNet with frame semantics from FrameNet and the definition of multifunctional relations between the verbs and the noun classes representing the selectional restrictions imposed on their participants. I also advance a number of observations on the interaction between syntax and semantics with reference to the behavior of Bulgarian verbs of contact, their arguments and their ontological place in the hierarchy of the BulNet structure. As the proposed analysis is based on multilingual resources such as WordNet and FrameNet some of the observations may also be useful for other languages and may contribute to the implementation of NLP applications aimed at automatic semantic analysis, word sense disambiguation, language understanding and generation, machine translation, etc.

Acknowledgments

The research presented in this paper is carried out as part of the scientific programme under the project *Enriching the Semantic Network Wordnet with Semantic Frames* funded by the Bulgarian National Science Fund (Grant Agreement No. KP-06-N50/1 of 2020).

References

C. F. Baker and C. Fellbaum. 2009. Wordnet and FrameNet as complementary resources for annotation. In *Proceedings of the Third Linguistic Annotation Workshop (LAW III)*, pages 125–129.

C. F. Baker, Ch.J. Fillmore, and John B. Lowe. 1998. The berkeley framenet project. *COLINGACL '98: Proceedings of the Conference. Montreal, Canada*, pages 86–90.

M. Brysbaert and A. Biemiller. 2017. Test-based age-of-acquisition norms for 44 thousand English word meanings. *Behavior Research Methods*, 49:1520–1523.

M. Dimitrova-Vulchanova and R. Dekova. 2009. On the encoding of lexical information: Events and their lexicalization in English and Bulgarian. *Bulgarian Language*, LVI:84–96.

C. Fellbaum. 1990. English verbs as a semantic net. *International Journal of Lexicography*, 3:278–301.

C. Fellbaum. 1999. *WordNet: an Electronic Lexical Database*. MIT Press, Cambridge.

Ch. Fillmore. 1970. The grammar of hitting and breaking. *R. A. Jacobs, P. A. Rosenbaum (Eds.), Readings in English Transformational Grammar*, pages 120–133.

H. Gao. 2001. Notions of motion and contact for physical contact verbs. *eds Holmer A., Svantesson J., Viberg A. Proceedings of the 18th Scandinavian Conference of Linguistics*, 2:193–209.

H. Gao and Ch. Cheng. 2003. Verbs of contact by impact in English and their equivalents in Mandarin Chinese. *Language and Linguistics*, 4.3:485—-508.

Al. Juffs. 1996. *Learnability and the Lexicon. Theories and Second Language Acquisition Research*. John Benjamin, Amsterdam.

S. Koeva. 2010. Bulgarian wordnet - current state, applications and prospects. *Bulgarian-American Dialogues*, pages 120–132.

S. Koeva. 2020. Towards a semantic network enriched with a variety of semantic relations. *Semantic Relations and Conceptual Frames, Koeva, S. (ed.)*, pages 7–20.

S. Koeva and E. Doychev. 2022. Ontology supported frame classification. *Proceedings of the Fifth International Conference Computational Linguistics in Bulgaria*, pages 203–214.

S. Koeva, I. Stoyanova, S. Leseva, T. Dimitrova, R. Dekova, and E. Tarpomanova. 2012. The Bulgarian National Corpus: Theory and practice in corpus design. *Journal of Language Modelling*, pages 65–110.

H. Kukova. 2020. Verbs for communication, frame elements and semantic restrictions (on BulNet synsets). *Proceedings of the International Annual Conference of the Institute for Bulgarian Language (Sofia, 2020)*, 2:233–241.

S. Leseva, I. Stoyanova, H. Kukova, and M. Todorova. 2018. Integrating subcategorization information in wordnet's relational structure. *Bulgarian Language*, 2:13–40.

S. Leseva, I. Stoyanova, M. Todorova, and H. Kukova. 2019. A theoretical overview of conceptual frames and semantic restrictions on frame elements. *Linguistique Balkanique*, LVIII(2):172–186.

S. Leseva, I. Stoyanova, M. Todorova, and H. Kukova. 2020. A semantic description of the combinability between verbs and nouns (on material from Bulgarian and English). *Chujdoezikovo obuchenie*, 47:115–128.

S. Leseva, I. Stoyanova, M. Todorova, and H. Kukova. 2021. Putting pieces together: Predicate-argument relations and selectional preferences. *Koeva, S. (ed.) Towards a Semantic Network Enriched with a Variety of Semantic Relations*.

B. Levin. 1993. *English verb classes and alternations: a preliminary investigation*. The University of Chicago Press, Chicago.

G. A. Miller. 1995. Wordnet: a lexical database for English. *Communications of the ACM*, 38(11):39—-41.

G. A. Miller, R. Beckwith, D. Gross C. Fellbaum, and K. Miller. 1990. Introduction to wordnet: an on-line lexical database. *International journal of lexicography*, 3(4):235–244.

J. Ruppenhofer, M. Ellsworth, M. R. L. Petruck, C. R. Johnson, C. F. Baker, and J. Scheffczyk. 2016. *FrameNet II: Extended Theory and Practice*. International Computer Science Institute, Berkeley, California.

I. Stoyanova and S. Leseva. 2020. Beyond lexical and semantic resources: Linking WordNet with FrameNet and enhancing synsets with conceptual frames. *Koeva, S. (ed.) Towards a Semantic Network Enriched with a Variety of Semantic Relations*, pages 21–48.

I. Stoyanova and S. Leseva. 2021. Semantic description of verbs for change and hierarchical organization of conceptual frames. In *Proceedings International Annual Conference of the Institute of Bulgarian Language "Prof. Lubomir Andreychin" (compilers – S. Koeva, M. Stamenov)*, volume 2, pages 76–85.

M. A. Todorova, T. Dimitrova, and V. Stefanova. 2022. Research on the basic verbal vocabulary in Bulgarian for students in the initial stage of education through online games. *Pedagogika-Pedagogy*, XCIV:896–913.

Appraisal Theory and the Annotation of Speaker-Writer Engagement

Min Dong
School of Foreign Languages
Beihang University
PR China
mdong@buaa.edu.cn

Alex Chengyu Fang
Department of Linguistics and Translation
City University of Hong Kong
Hong Kong SAR
acfang@cityu.edu.hk

Abstract

In this work, we address the annotation of language resources through the application of the engagement network in appraisal theory. This work represents an attempt to extend the advances in studies of speech and dialogue acts to encompass the latest notion of stance negotiations in discourse, between the writer and other sources. This type of phenomenon has become especially salient in contemporary media communication and requires some timely research to address emergent requirement. We shall first of all describe the engagement network as proposed by Martin and White (2005) and then discuss the issue of multi-subjectivity. We shall then propose and describe a bi-step procedure towards better annotation before discussing the benefits of engagement network in the assessment of speaker-writer stance. We shall finally discuss issues of annotation consistency and reliability.

Keywords: annotation consistency, multi-subjectivity, engagement, appraisal theory, media discourse

1. Introduction

Engagement in appraisal research is concerned with sourcing opinions and the speaker's alignment with respect to them, i.e. the way in which the speaker positions him/herself with regard to these opinions as well as hypothetical responses from the audience (Martin & White 2005: 91-134). It provides the resources through which speakers construe their point of view and take stances towards others' opinions, including all items by which the textual or authorial voice is positioned intersubjectively (Read et al 2007: 94). Significantly, the Engagement system has shifted the focus of appraisal research from static investigation of personal attitudinal meaning to a position highlighting the dynamic processes of meaning negotiation between interlocutors (Huan 2016: 4). Hunston (2011: 35) further argues that due to the intertextual feature of discourse, the sourcing of evaluation is dialogic, being highly susceptible to conditioning by the co-text in which it occurs, which makes it more difficult for a reader to isolate a single voice for (dis)agreement. For example, in the rhetorical question of example (1), the writer reports an evaluation from the source of *scientists* that the mutation of the virus is *possible*, while the writer views it as *unlikely*. Evidently, the sentence construes a contrast of opinions between the authorial voice and the attributee.

[1] *Why should scientists suddenly <u>fear that the H5N1 virus is likely to mutate soon, and become transmissible among humans</u>, when it has been around for at least 50 years?*

According to the two overarching sourcing types, the dialogistic positionings are classified into two general semantic domains of Expand and Contract. As visualized in Figure 1, Expand is subdivided into Entertain and Attribute, through which an utterance actively makes allowances for alternative positions and voices, while Contract subdivided into Disclaim and Proclaim, which act to challenge, fend off or restrict the scope of such. More specifically, under Disclaim, the sub-domain of Deny means rejecting a position, and in the option of Counter, while the alternative position has been recognised, it is held not to apply (Martin & White 2005: 117). Under Proclaim, three options are involved (Martin & White 2005: 120): Concur which overtly announces the journalist as agreeing with, or having the same knowledge as the public audience; Pronounce which concerns explicit authorial intrusion into the dialogue; and Endorse by which propositions sourced to external evidences are construed by the authorial voice as correct, valid, undeniable or otherwise maximally warrantable (Martin & White 2005: 121, 126).

In the case of Expand, the proposition is overtly grounded in either the contingent, individual subjectivity of the speaker/writer in relation to evidentials and epistemic modals, i.e. Entertain, or in the contingent subjectivity of the quoted source with regard to attribution, i.e. Attribute (White 2012: 61). By Entertain, we mean the authorial voice indicates that its position is but one of a number of possible positions and therefore, to greater or lesser degrees, makes dialogic space for those possibilities. Within Attribute, while through the Acknowledge option the speaker simply acknowledges the attributtee's voice as one of a range of possible voices without making a choice of preferred voice, the Distance sub-domain explicitly detaches the writer from responsibility for what is being reported, therefore maximising the space for dialogic alternatives (Martin & White 2005: 113), as shown in example (1).

Proceedings of the 19th Joint ACL - ISO Workshop on Interoperable Semantic Annotation, pages 18–26
June 20, 2023. ©2023 Association for Computational Linguistics

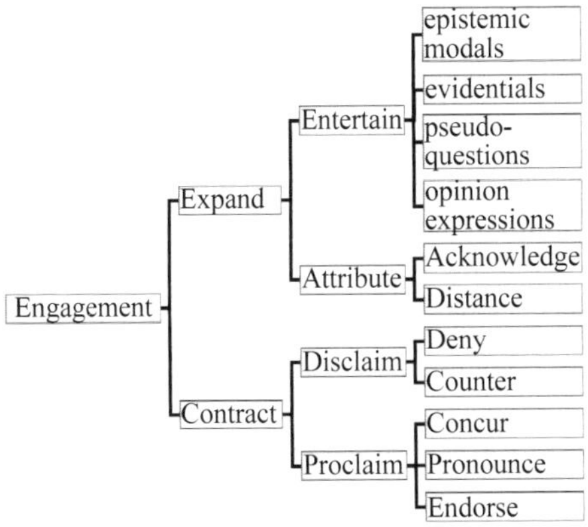

Fig 1: Engagement in Martin&White (2005: 134)

In addition, from a dialogistic perspective, White (2012: 64) proposes the notion of dialogistic association to refer to the positioning of the authorial voice re the attributed proposition. It is not hard to see that the above three options of Acknowledge, Distance and Endorse fit into the framework of dialogistic association, as depicted in Figure 2. To specify, Acknowledge is taxonomised as unmarked or neutral, that is, the author presents the attributed proposition for the reader's consideration, either possibly indicating a dialogic stance on the part of the attributed voice or not (White 2012: 66), while Distance as Disassociating, namely the author "stands away from" the attributed proposition, and Endorse as Associating, viz, the author "stands with" the attributed proposition, construing it as a given.

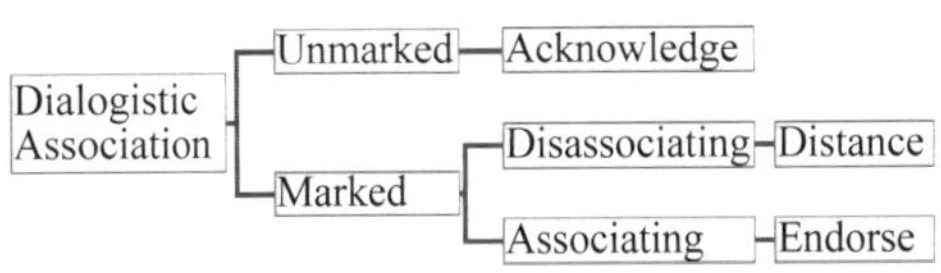

Fig. 2: Dialogistic association (White 2012: 64)

Evaluation is dependent on context, which can be defined as the immediate environment of the co-occurring words and structures (Hunston 2011: 17). As a matter of fact, appraisal is much more complex and requires a multitude of different considerations that often extend beyond the current text. Methodologically, Engagement is taxonomised based on discourse semantic categories which are used to label a stretch of discourse by referring to as much of the context and meaning of the discourse as necessary (Martin & White 2005). These conditions, however, have not been discussed in any detail in the literature, thus classifying expressions of Engagement, which is a fundamentally subjective exercise, has not received any clearly laid out consensus. As Macken-Horarik & Isaac (2014: 81) have observed, evaluation "resists enclosure in analytical boxes and frustrates the 'either-or' distinctions that are central to the [Appraisal] system network". Yet, as has been widely believed, unequivocal choices are an inescapable part of the process of text annotation.

Being difficult and subject, the task of classifying Engagement expressions based on the categories provided by the Appraisal model poses several conceptual and methodological challenges. Different interpretations for an expression are often equally plausible, and multiple category labels valid. The more fine-grained the analysis is, the more problematic and subjective classification choices become (Read & Carroll 2012). As noted by Macken-Horarik & Isaac (2014: 88), one strategy to cope with this type of ambiguities is to allow for double or multiple coding. Rather than annotating expressions with one single category label, we can, when necessary, apply two or more. However, there are several drawbacks to this approach (Fuoli 2018). Most notably, the degree of subjectivity and inconsistency involved in the annotation process grows substantially, as the number of possible choices for each item increases. The number and variety of highly subjective decisions that, as discussed above, are involved in the task of identifying and classifying expressions of Engagement may represent a challenge to achieving acceptable standards of reliability, replicability and transparency.

Context-specific definitions and guidelines are in most cases necessary to be explicitly formulated and made available to other analysts. In this article, we address the issue of stance nouns and their annotation according to the Engagement network of Appraisal Theory. This type of phenomenon has become especially salient in contemporary media communication and requires some timely research to address emergent requirement. Our work was based on stance nouns (StNs) retrieved from a corpus of British media and a corpus of Chinese media, aiming to identify differences and similarities across the two discourse groups. This work is taken as a pioneering effort towards a framework of annotation that is suitable for consistent, computationally trackable application.

2. A description of corpora as primary data

The term "stance noun" refers to the nominal expression of the writer's point of view towards the content specified in the complement fragment (Biber et al 1999: 986; Charles 2007; Jiang & Hyland 2015). According to Biber et al (1999: 645-649), Schmid (2000: 57, 59) and Jiang & Hyland (2015), there is the strongest tendency for noun phrases to take complement *that*-clauses in different registers, which generally provide only semantic equivalence of what the head nouns are. The present study is well justified to focus on stance nouns ensued by appositive *that*-clauses, i.e. StN + *that*, the reliable syntactic test for identifying stance nouns with minimal reliance on expert judgement in borderline cases.

The primary data comes from two comparable corpora of media English texts (Fang et al 2012). The resources comprise *Corpus of British Media English* (CBME) and *Corpus of Chinese Media English* (CCME), each of a total size of about one million word tokens. The two comparable corpora follow an identical design constituting three media types, namely, newspapers, magazines and the Internet. For each media type, five text categories are identified, including news, editorial, society, culture and arts, and business. The pre-designated corpus size is equally distributed across the three media types and the five text categories.

The two corpora were grammatically tagged for part-of-speech (POS) information using AUTASYS (Fang 1996) and then syntactically parsed for detailed structural information using the Survey Parser (Fang 2006). For every parsed tree, each node is regarded as a function-category pair and annotated as such. The subject NP is annotated as SU NP, the former indicating the syntactic function, i.e. subject, and the latter the syntactic category, that is, noun phrase. The *that*-clause is annotated as APPOS CL, indicating the presence of a clause (CL) functioning as an apposition (APPOS) of the antecedent noun. The two corpora were automatically parsed and then manually checked and corrected where necessary. Sentences containing StN+*that* constructions were identified through manual validation based on the criteria of semantic equivalence between the head noun and the proposition expressed by the APPO CL *that*-clause. Consider

[2] He said that Mr Fisher had not alerted Mr Brooker or their record company when he decided to take action, "with the **result** *that they could not prepare themselves to meet the claim*". <#British/web/social>

In example (2), *result* is identifiable as stance noun due to its encapsulation of the proposition in the appositive *that*-clause. It should be noted in N + *that*-clause constructions, *that* functions as a subordinate conjunction rather than a relative pronoun leading a relative clause. Compare

[3] And if people keep coming back to discuss it, that's the best **result** **that we can have*, he says. <#British/web/culture>

In this sentence, the head noun *result* acts as object in the relative postmodifying *that*-clause, being offered with some descriptive information. This is in sharp contrast with what happens in example (2) in which the stance noun *result* plays no syntactic role inside the appositive *that*-clause as its complete content is presented in the latter.

Table 1: Stance nouns in CBME and CCME

	StN Sent	StN Tokens	StN Types
CBME	783	846	190
CCME	361	406	115
Total	1144	1252	231

It should be noted the present study takes a corpus-driven view of language which focuses on individual wordforms rather than abstractions such as lemmas (Sinclair 1991: 44-51). We took plural forms of StNs into due consideration, systematically searching potential plural forms of StNs and including valid instances into the quantitative data, such as *concerns, signs, reports*. Some basic information about our primary data is summarized in Table 1. We observe that British English employs roughly twice as many StNs in terms of the number of sentences with StN+*that* construction, the number of StN tokens, and the number of StN types. These striking differences in the use of StNs across the two groups of professional writers of English might be further reflected in the Engagement annotation results.

3. Annotation and results

The annotation was carried out by one annotator and in three phases: annotation of Engagement contextual factors, annotation of dialogic expansion and contraction categories, and annotation of neutral, disassociating, and associating dialogistic options. Six factors were considered: source type, functional class of stance noun, type of information expressed in appositive *that*-clause, additional expansive marker, additional contractive marker and additional disassociating marker. The six factors are listed with corresponding values in Table 2. Options of the first three factors were manually annotated in phase 1, on the 783 and 361 sentences containing StN + *that* constructions, identified in the two corpora of British and Chinese media English texts.

Table 2: Description of six factors for phase 1 annotation

Factors	Values	
Source type (Martin & White 2005)	Authorial	
	Non-authorial	
	Hard proof	
Functional class of stance nouns (Jiang and Hyland 2015)	Event	Event/ Manner noun
	Evidentiality	Discourse/ Cognition/ Relation/ Quality/ Manner noun
	Modality	Status noun

Expansive marker (Coffin 2006)	Such as	hedge, modal verb/ adverb/ noun, possessive + evidential noun, reported speech
Contractive marker (Coffin 2006)	Such as	negative marker, second person pronoun, first person pronoun, unmodalised affirmative clause
Disassociating marker (Coffin 2006)	Such as	verb of negative attitude, negative marker, adjective of negative attitude
Type of information expressed in appositive *that*-clause (Schmid 2000; Jiang and Hyland 2015)	Opinion	Discourse/ Cognition/ Relation/ Quality/ Manner/ Status noun
	Event	Hard proof/ Neutral fact event noun, Manner noun

The result of phase 1 annotation is summarised in Table 3. It is observable that both the British and Chinese writers make frequent use of cognition StNs, but the former mostly for the authorial source while the latter mostly for the non-authorial source. In addition, the loglikelihood ratio test suggests that the British journalists tend to make heavy use of discourse StNs (LR=4.913228, $p<0.05$) across non-authorial sources, whereas the Chinese colleagues prefer the use of event StNs (LR=-13.652045, $p<0.001$) across the authorial and hard proof sources.

Table 3: Phase 1 annotation result for the corpora of CBME and CCME: Different classes of stance noun, types of *that*-clause and source types

stance noun	***that*-clause**	**Source type**	**CBME**		**CCME**	
			Freq	**Prop (%)**	**Freq**	**Prop (%)**
Cognition	Opinion	Authorial	164	19.4	39	9.6
		Non-authorial	120	13.9	94	23.0
		Subtotal	*284*	*33.6*	*133*	*32.8*
Discourse	Opinion	Authorial	55	6.5	22	5.4
		Non-authorial	183	21.6	65	15.8
Subtotal			*238*	*28.1*	*87*	*21.4*
Event	Event	Authorial	75	8.9	50	12.3
		Non-authorial	47	5.5	17	4.1
		hard proof + Non-authorial	12	1.4	24	5.8
		hard proof	55	6.5	47	11.6
		Subtotal	*189*	*22.3*	*138*	*34*
Manner	Event	Authorial	--	--	6	1.5
	Opinion	Non-authorial	1	0.1	2	0.4
		Authorial	1	0.1	--	--
		Subtotal	*2*	*0.2*	*8*	*2*
Quality	Opinion	Authorial	2	0.2	--	--
		Subtotal	*2*	*0.2*	--	--
Relation	Opinion	Authorial	3	0.3	--	--
		Non-authorial	25	2.9	4	0.9
		Subtotal	*28*	*3.3*	*4*	*1*
Status	Opinion	Authorial	71	8.4	20	4.9
		Non-authorial	32	3.8	16	4.0
		Subtotal	*103*	*12.2*	*36*	*8.9*
		Total	*846*	*100*	*406*	*100*

In phase 2 the contextual factors of additional contractive marker and additional expansive marker were annotated. We summarise the contractive and expansive contextual patterns observed in the corpora of CBME and CCME in Table 4. On the basis of these contractive and expansive contextual patterns identified, Engagement categories correspondingly in the domains of Contract and Expand were annotated. The results are summarised in Table 5.

Table 4: Phase 2 annotation results for CBME and CCME: Summary of contractive and expansive contextual patterns

Dialogic contextual patterns in terms of contraction and expansion	**CBME**		**CCME**	
	Freq	**%**	**Freq**	**%**
Contractive contextual patterns	**220**	**26**	**158**	**38.9**
hard proof event noun	115	13.6	58	14.3
neutral fact event noun + Authorial	54	6.4	11	2.7
negative clause + Authorial	26	3.1	11	2.7
unmodalised/ deontically modalised affirmative clause + Authorial	11	1.3	58	14.3
second person pronoun/reader + Authorial	5	0.6	--	--
first person pronoun + Authorial	8	0.9	7	1.7

rhetorical question as negative clause + Authorial	1	0.1	2	0.5
Expansive contextual patterns	**626**	**74**	**248**	**61.1**
evidential opinion noun + Authorial	166	19.6	34	8.4
non-authorial + evidential opinion noun	133	15.7	61	15
non-authorial + evidential opinion noun in plural	50	5.9	27	6.7
modal opinion noun + Authorial	75	8.9	20	4.9
possessive + evidential opinion noun	40	4.7	17	4.2
neutral fact event non/ modal opinion noun in reported speech	31	3.7	32	7.9
non-authorial premodifier + evidential opinion noun	19	2.2	9	2.2
evidential opinion noun + Authorial + partial negative "little"	5	0.6	--	--
non-authorial + modal opinion noun	--	--	6	1.5
non-authorial + hard proof event noun + modal verb	--	--	2	0.5
hard proof event noun + Authorial in conditional clause	3	0.4	--	--
hard proof event noun + epistemically modalised clause + Authorial	2	0.2	--	--
neutral fact event noun + Authorial in modalised clause	1	0.1	--	--
neutral fact event noun + Authorial in subjunctive mood clause	1	0.1	--	--
non-authorial + evidential opinion noun + negative attitude	36	4.3	9	2.2
non-authorial + evidential opinion noun in plural + negative attitude	29	3.4	14	3.4
possessive + evidential opinion noun + negative attitude	26	3.1	5	1.2
non-authorial premodifier + evidential opinion noun + negative attitude	7	0.8	7	1.7
modal opinion noun + negative attitude in reported speech	1	0.1	5	1.2
non-authorial + modal opinion noun + negative attitude	1	0.1	--	--
Total	*846*	*100*	*406*	*100*

Table 5: Phase 2 annotation result for the corpora of CBME and CCME: Summary of engagement categories in terms of dialogical orientation

Dialogical orientation	**Engagement category**	**CBME**		**CCME**	
		Freq	**Prop (%)**	**Freq**	**Prop (%)**
Expansion	Acknowledge	273	32.3	154	37.9
	Entertain	253	29.9	54	13.3
	Distance	100	11.8	40	9.8
	Subtotal	*626*	*74*	*248*	*61.1*
Contraction	Endorse	86	10.2	68	16.7
	Pronounce	71	8.4	72	17.7
	Deny	62	7.3	15	3.7
	Counter	1	0.1	3	0.7
	Subtotal	*220*	*26.0*	*158*	*38.9*
	Total	*846*	*100.0*	*406*	*100.0*

As indicated in Table 4, both the British and Chinese journalists prefer to expand dialogic space, for which the three contextual patterns of "evidential opinion noun + Authorial", "Non-authorial + evidential opinion noun" and "Non-authorial + evidential opinion noun in plural" are commonly most frequently used. In addition, the former also make heavy use of "modal opinion noun + Authorial", while the latter also of "neutral fact event/ modal opinion noun in reported speech". More notably, we observe a visibly reduction of expansion in Chinese media coupled with a salient increase in contraction, with a significant difference between the two as suggested by the loglikelihood ratio test (expansion, LR=6.707140, p<0.01; contraction, LR=-14.528171, p<0.001). This difference may lend itself to the suggestion that in Chinese media English texts, while the meanings construe a dialogistic backdrop of other voices and other value positions, the Chinese media are inclined to exclude or constrain certain dialogic alternatives. On the part of the British media, however, they tend to put the current proposition into play in a way which opens up the space for the dialogic alternatives. In other words, in intersubjective terms of evaluation, the British group can be said to be more discursive while the Chinese group more assertive of a particular stance, most probably an official one (Zhao 2008).

A loglikelihood ratio test of the data presented in Table 5 further shows that within the domain of expansion, the British journalists favour the option of Entertain (LR=34.385400, p<0.001). This finding may suggest that the British media prefer to dominate the discourse with their own voice while constructing meanings which indicate that the authorial position is but one of a number of possible positions. At the same time, the two journalistic groups exhibit no significant difference in the use of the other two expansive options of Acknowledge and Distance, quite an expectable result in view of the commonly held journalism ideology of neutrality and objectivity. Within the domain of contraction, the Chinese journalists favour the option of Pronounce (LR=-19.592595, p<0.001), suggestive of their inclination to signal the explicit authorial intrusion into the negotiation in text. Differently, the British media tend to make the choice of

Deny (LR=6.449762, $p<0.05$), suggestive of their preference for constructing meanings which serve to reject a position, being maximally contractive. In addition, the Chinese media also skew towards the choice of Endorse (LR=-9.195267, $p<0.01$), indicating their preference for the use of external evidences as sources responsible for the propositions being advanced by the authorial or other voice as undeniable or maximally warrantable. Significantly, these differing preferences exhibited by the two groups of journalistic professionals can provide empirical support for the idea that the western media is more discursive in media reality construction whereas the Chinese media is more assertive in news event narration (Huan 2016).

It is noteworthy that in Engagement system, the boundaries between dialogic expansion and contraction are not always clear-cut, especially when it comes to the sub-categories of Entertain (sub-domain within Expand) and Proclaim (sub-domain within Contract). Certain markers of Engagement may be interpreted as instances of Entertain in certain contexts, but of Proclaim in others. Compare

[4] Compounding the situation was the **fact** *that banking institutions' loaning services only reached 37 percent of farmer households*. <#Chinese/magazine/editorial>

[5] His tenure there is generally agreed to have been particularly successful, despite the **fact** *that he used to have the reputation of being a difficult and wayward man*. <#British/magazine/arts>

It is shown that in example (4) the noun *fact* occurs in an unmodalised affirmative clause, marking the writer's seemingly objective stance towards the verifiable state of affairs encapsulated in the appositive *that*-clause. It is justifiably annotated as Pronounce. In example (5) *fact* however, occurs in the *despite* prepositional phrase, being contrasted with the information contained in the main clause and marking the author's judgment of certainty towards the complement proposition. It is arguably an instance of Entertain.

Additionally, the distinction of two options in Expand, i.e. Entertain and Attribute, also poses visible challenges. Consider

[6] GUO Qiang, general manager of Shanghai Zhongcheng Digital Technology Co., Ltd., has been on edge due to declining orders, but is breathing a little easier following **news** *that the tax rebate rate for exports of mechanical and electrical products is being raised*. <#Chinese/magazine/business>

In this example, the noun *news*, carrying no determiner, can be annotated as Entertain through interpreting the source of the complement proposition as the writer or alternatively as Acknowledge through attributing it to an additional source which is not specified in the text. According to Sinclair (1986) and Martin & White (2005: 72), normally the speaker/writer is interpreted as the source of a proposition and takes responsibility for its truth, i.e. averral, unless it is projected as the speech or thought of an additional source (some other person or entity), i.e. attribution. In this article we are thus motivated to analyse example (6) as fitting into the category of Entertain. Moreover, when stance nouns are used in plural form, they are annotated as attributed to unspecified non-authorial sources in text, as illustrated in (7) below.

[7] THE KLF have announced a temporary departure from the music business in the wake of **rumours** *that the band is to be permanently dissolved*. <#British/magazine/arts>

In phase 3 the additional disassociating markers, the sixth contextual factor as listed in Table 2, were annotated. We summarise the associating, dialogically neutral and disassociating contextual patterns observed in the corpora of CBME and CCME in Table 6. On the basis of these dialogistic association patterns identified, Engagement categories correspondingly in the domains of Dialogistic unmarked/ neutral (Acknowledge), Associating (Endorse) and Disassociating (Distance) were annotated. The results are summarised in Table 7.

As shown in Table 6, the British and Chinese journalistic writers both tend to associate the positions being advanced in text with non-authorial voices and sources of external evidences. Additionally, the loglikelihood ratio test suggests that a significant difference between the two groups (British 54.3% vs. Chinese 64.5%, LR=-4.934618, $p<0.05$). This observation may be linked to the preferred choice of associating contextual patterns by the Chinese writers (LR=-9.195267, $p<0.01$), including "hard proof event noun" and "relational verb clause + Authorial", indicative of the author's stance of "standing with" the attributed proposition sourced to external evidences and therefore construing them as givens. Differently, the British group prefer to make dialogically neutral choices in the sense of being inclined to engage interactively with attributed voices and positions, therefore reclaiming responsibility for the truth of the propositions expressed in the appositive *that*-clauses.

According to the data presented in Table 7, the two groups of journalistic writers commonly favour the dialogically unmarked option of Acknowledge and the disassociating option of Distance. In other words, they are both inclined to present the propositions sourced to attribution voices for the reader's consideration, and also to stand away from the proposition attributed to the non-authorial voices. With regard to the choice of Endorse, however, the Chinese journalists make a significantly heavier use than the British (LR=-9.195267, p<0.01), suggesting that the Chinese group are more concerned with the factuality and objectivity of what is reported in news text by resort to external evidences which help to construe propositions as correct and valid (Huan 2016).

Table 6: Phase 3 annotation results for CBME and CCME: Summary of dialogically neutral, associating and disassociating contextual patterns

Engagement contextual patterns in terms of dialogistic association	**CBME**		**CCME**	
	Freq	**%**	**Freq**	**%**
Associating contextual patterns (Endorse)	**86**	**10.2**	**68**	**16.7**
hard proof event noun	86	10.2	57	14
relational verb clause + authorial	--	--	11	2.7
Dialogically neutral contextual patterns (Acknowledge)	**273**	**32.3**	**154**	**37.9**
Non-authorial + evidential opinion noun	133	15.7	61	15
Non-authorial + evidential opinion noun in plural	50	5.9	27	6.7
Possessive + evidential opinion noun	40	4.7	17	4.2
neutral fact event/ modal opinion noun in reported speech	**31**	3.6	32	7.9
Non-authorial premodifier + evidential opinion noun	19	2.2	9	2.2
Non-authorial + modal opinion noun	--	--	6	1.5
Non-authorial + hard proof event noun + modal verb	--	--	2	0.5
Disassociating contextual patterns (Distance)	**100**	**11.8**	**40**	**9.8**
Non-authorial + evidential opinion noun + negative attitude	36	4.3	9	2.2
Non-authorial + evidential opinion noun in plural + negative attitude	29	3.4	14	3.4
Possessive + evidential opinion noun + negative attitude	26	3.1	5	1.2
Non-authorial premodifier + evidential opinion noun + negative attitude	7	0.8	7	1.7
modal opinion noun + negative attitude in reported speech	1	0.1	5	1.2
Non-authorial + modal opinion noun + negative attitude	1	0.1	--	--
Total	*459*	*54.3*	*262*	*64.5*

Next, we attempt to investigate whether and how the contextual factors annotated in Phase 1, including source types, types of stance nouns and information expressed in appositive *that*-clause, are associated with the annotation of engagement categories in Phases 2 and 3. For this purpose, we present the distribution of sour types across engagement categories in the two corpora of CBME and CCME in Table 7.

Table 7: Distribution of source types across engagement categories in CBME and CCME

Engagement category	**Source type**	**CBME**		**CCME**	
		Freq	**Prop (%)**	**Freq**	**Prop (%)**
Acknowledge	Non-authorial	273	32.3	154	37.9
Distance	Non-authorial	100	11.8	40	9.9
Entertain	Authorial	253	29.9	52	12.8
	Authorial + Hard proof	--	--	2	0.5
Counter	Authorial	1	0.1	1	0.2
	Hard proof + Non-authorial	--	--	2	0.5
Deny	Authorial	46	5.4	14	3.4
	Hard proof + Non-authorial	16	1.9	1	0.2
Endorse	Hard proof + Non-authorial	38	4.5	23	5.7
	Hard proof	48	5.7	45	11.1
Pronounce	Authorial	71	8.4	72	17.7

As expounded above, the British writers prefer the expansive option of Entertain and the contractive option of Deny, while the Chinese counterparts favour the contractive/ associating option of Endorse, and also Pronounce. As the data in Table 9 indicates, this finding may be explained by the former's preference for the authorial voice in opening up the possibility of dialogic alternatives in addition to the heavy use of non-authorial sources. Furthermore, within the domain of contraction, the British media tend to exploit the authorial voice to reject a proposition as one means of the persuasive endeavour of media reality construction. The Chinese media, however, are inclined to deploy the authorial voice or external evidences to explicitly claim the writer's stance towards the objectivity of news story telling, making visibly more narrative efforts.

Table 8: Distribution of types of stance nouns across engagement categories in each of the two corpora of CBME and CCME

Engagement category	Type of StN	CBME		CCME	
		Freq	Prop (%)	Freq	Prop (%)
Acknowledge	Cognition	100	11.8	75	18.5
	Discourse	107	12.6	45	11.1
	Event	12	1.4	15	3.7
	Manner	1	0.1	2	0.5
	Relation	24	2.8	3	0.7
	Status	29	3.4	14	3.4
Counter	Event	1	0.1	3	0.7
Deny	Cognition	19	2.2	8	2
	Discourse	4	0.5	5	1.2
	Event	34	4	2	0.5
	Relation	1	0.1	--	--
	Status	4	0.5	--	--
Distance	Cognition	20	2.4	16	3.9
	Discourse	76	9	20	4.9
	Relation	1	0.1	1	0.2
	Status	3	0.4	2	0.5
	Manner	--	--	1	0.2
Endorse	Event	86	10.2	68	16.7
Entertain	Cognition	136	16.1	17	4.2
	Discourse	41	4.8	13	3.2
	Event	4	0.5	2	0.5
	Manner	1	0.1	2	0.5
	Quality	2	0.2	--	--
	Relation	2	0.2	--	--
	Status	67	7.9	20	4.9
Pronounce	Cognition	9	1.1	17	4.2
	Discourse	10	1.2	4	1
	Event	52	6.1	48	11.8
	Manner	--	--	3	0.7

As indicated in Table 3, each of the two groups of writers tends to make heavy use of cognition StNs. Besides, the Chinese media prefer the use of event StNs, whereas the British media favour the use of discourse StNs. According to the data in Table 8, it may be further argued that the British journalists prefer the choice of cognition StNs in association with the authorial voice to open up the dialogic space for alternatives, i.e. Entertain (LR=38.164356, $p<0.001$), while the Chinese counterparts favour to use this type of StNs in the context of explicitly marking the authorial intrusion into the dialogue, i.e. Pronounce (LR=-11.802792, $p<0.001$). In addition, the Chinese media' preference for the contractive option of Pronounce and Endorse can be explained by their preferred choice of event StNs across the authorial voice for the former (LR=-10.406200, $p<0.01$) and hard proof source for the latter (LR=-9.195267, $p<0.01$). However, the British media's preference for the use of discourse StNs seems to have no visible link to the choice of engagement options, as the two groups do not exhibit significant difference in the choice of Acknowledge and Distance. Furthermore, the British media's preference for the choice of the contractive option of Deny cannot be connected to the use of particular type of StNs. This result seems to suggest that the contextual factors of the type of StN and the type of appositive *that*-clause have no observable association with the choice of engagement options. These findings provide a further empirical support for the methodology expounded in this study, namely annotation of contractive/ expansive and dialogistic neutral/ associating/ disassociating contextual patterns.

5. Conclusion

In this article, we address the issue of stance nouns and their annotation according to the engagement network of Appraisal Theory. Our results show that the two groups indeed demonstrate significant differences from the engagement-based perspective, in terms of stance types, source and types, and discourse strategy in terms of expansion and contraction, and also in dialogistic association terms. While the results have demonstrated the usefulness of Appraisal Theory in empirical terms when applied to discourse analysis, the multi-subjectivity nature of contemporary media discourse has also raised a challenge to the formation of a consistent and reliable framework of analysis. Our future work will be focused on a feasibility study to test whether a subsequent annotator's manual, informed by the current study, can be compiled and used to produce annotation results meeting the requirement of acceptable inter-annotator consistency. This is not only crucial for improving reliability and replicability, but also for ensuring transparency, i.e. allowing others to trace and fully understand the annotation process and correctly and critically interpret and assess the results. Moreover, by disclosing the annotation criteria, we enable other researchers to contribute to their improvement, and, ultimately, to a progressive and collaborative development of the APPRAISAL model.

Acknowledgements

This work is supported in part by Research Grant Nos. 7020036 and 9360115 received from City University of Hong Kong, NSSF Grant No. 22BYY009 received from the National Office for Philosophy and Social Sciences of China and Grant No. 18JDYYA005 received from the Municipal Office for Philosophy and Social Sciences of Beijing.

References

Biber, D. Johansson, S. Leech, G. Conrad, S. and Finegan, E. (1999). *Longman Grammar of Spoken and Written English.* Harlow: Pearson Education.

Charles, M. (2007). Argument or evidence? Disciplinary variation in the use of the Noun *that* pattern in stance construction. *English for Specific Purposes*, 26: 203-218.

Coffin, C. (2006). *Historical Discourse: The Language of Time, Cause and Evaluation.* London; New York: Continuum.

Fang, A.C. (1996). AUTASYS: Automatic tagging and cross-tagset mapping. In S. Greenbaum (Ed.), *Comparing English Worldwide: The International Corpus of English.* Oxford: Oxford University Press, pp. 110-124.

Fang, A.C. (2006). Evaluating the performance of the Survey Parser with the NIST scheme. In A. Gelbukh (Ed.), LNCS: *Computational Linguistics and Intelligent Text Processing.* Berlin Heidelberg: Springer-Verlag, pp. 168-179.

Fang, A.C., Le, F. & Cao, J. (2012). A Comparative corpus of China and British Englishes. *Studies of Language and Linguistics*, 32(2): 113-127.

Fuoli, M. (2018). A stepwise method for annotating APPRAISAL. *Functions of Language*, 25(2): 229-258.

Huan, C. (2016). Journalistic engagement patterns and power relations: Corpus evidence from Chinese and Australian hard news reporting. *Discourse & Communication*, 10(2): 137-156.

Hunston, S. (2011). *Corpus approaches to evaluation: Phraseology and evaluative language*. New York: Routledge.

Jiang, F. & Hyland, K. (2015). "The fact that": Stance nouns in disciplinary writing. *Discourse Studies*, 17: 529-550.

Macken-Horarik, M. & Isaac, A. (2014). Appraising Appraisal. In G. Thompson & L. Alba-Juez (Eds.), *Evaluation in Context.* Amsterdam: Benjamins, pp. 67-92.

Martin, J. & White, P. (2005). *The Language of Evaluation: Appraisal in English.* New York: Palgrave Macmillan.

Read, J. & Carroll, J. (2012). Annotating expressions of Appraisal in English. *Language Resources and Evaluation*, 46(3). 421–447.

Read, J., Hope, D. & Carroll, J. (2007). Annotating expressions of appraisal in English. In *Proceedings of the Linguistic Annotation Workshop, ACL 2007*, pp. 93-100.

Schmid, H. J. (2000). *English Abstract Nouns as Conceptual Shells: From Corpus to Cognition.* Berlin: Mouton de Gruyter.

Sinclair, J. (1986). Fictional Worlds. In M Coulthard (Ed.). *Talking About Text: Studies Presented to David Brazil on his Retirement.* Birmingham: University of Birmingham, English Language Research, pp. 43-60.

Sinclair, J. (1991). *Corpus Concordance Collocation.* Oxford: Oxford University Press.

White, P. R. R. (2012). Exploring the axiological workings of "reporter voice" news stories– Attribution and attitudinal positioning. *Discourse, Context & Media*, 1: 57-67.

Zhao,Y. (2008) *Communication in China: Political Economy, Power, and Conflict.* Lanham, MD: Rowman & Littlefield Publishers.

metAMoRphosED: a graphical editor for Abstract Meaning Representation

Johannes Heinecke
Orange Innovation
2 avenue Pierre Marzin
F-22300 Lannion
johannes.heinecke@orange.com

Abstract

This paper presents a graphical editor for directed graphs, serialised in the PENMAN format, as used for annotations in Abstract Meaning Representation (AMR). The tool supports creation and modification of AMR graphs and other directed graphs, addition and deletion of instances, edges and literals, renaming of concepts, relations and literals, setting a "top node" and validation of the edited graph.

1 Introduction

Abstract Meaning Representation (AMR) is a semantic representation language designed to formalise the meaning of sentences or a set of sentences (Banarescu et al., 2013)[1]. Its motivation is to annotate semantic information like named entities, coreferences, word senses, semantic relations etc. However, it does not annotate meaning of natural language at the same degree as more complex frameworks such as the Discourse Representation Theory (Kamp and Reyle, 1993), as it does not mark number, semantic time, mode etc. Even though AMR has been explicitely devised for English and must not be considered as an interlingua, AMR is increasingly used to annotate sentences in languages other than English (Damonte and Cohen, 2018; Blloshmi et al., 2020; Uhrig et al., 2021; Heinecke and Shimorina, 2022). AMR graphs are directed graphs which contain concepts, instances, literals and labelled edges between instances and literals.

AMR uses concepts from PropBank (Kingsbury and Palmer, 2002; Palmer et al., 2005) where available (mainly verbal concepts), e.g., *bear-02* in figure 1, PropBank sense 2 for *bear*. Instances are indicated by a following "/", e.g., *p* being an instance of the concept *person*. `:ARG1` etc. mark relations. Literals (strings and numbers) lack an preceeding instance and "/" (c.f., *"Queen"* and *1926* in the example in figure 1).

```
(b / bear-02
    :ARG1 (p / person
        :name (n / name
            :op1 "Queen"
            :op2 "Elizabeth"))
    :time (d / date-entity
        :year 1926))
```

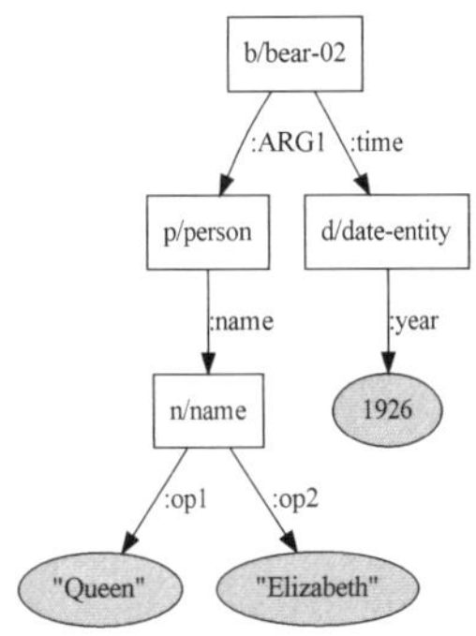

Figure 1: AMR graph for "Queen Elizabeth was born in 1926" in PENMAN format (above) and graphical visualisation

AMR data is available at the Linguistic Data Consortium (LDC) for English 2 :

- LDC2020T02: LDC general release AMR 3.0 (2020), with 59,255 sentences;
- LDC2017T10: LDC general release AMR 2.0 (2017), with 39,260 sentences.

The sentences of the test corpus of AMR 2.0 were translated by human translators into four languages (LDC2020T07: AMR 2.0, four translations of AMR 2.0 test set into Italian, Spanish, German, Chinese, 1371 sentences per language).[2]

[1] See also the project web site https://amr.isi.edu

[2] Corpora available at https://amr.isi.edu/download.html

Proceedings of the 19th Joint ACL - ISO Workshop on Interoperable Semantic Annotation, pages 27–32
June 20, 2023.

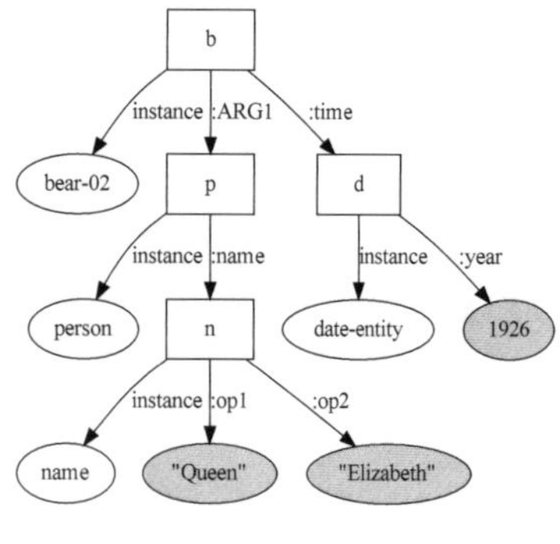

Figure 2: AMR graph of figure 1 with instances explicitely visualised

```
# ::id lpp_1943.293 ::date 2012-11-18...
# ::snt I answered , "eats anything ...
# ::save-date Thu Apr 18, 2013 ...
(a / answer-01
   :ARG0 (i / i)
   :ARG1 (e / eat-01
      :ARG1 (a2 / anything
         :ARG1-of (f / find-01
            :ARG0 (i2 / it)
            :location (r / reach-03
               :ARG0 i2)))))

# ::id lpp_1943.294 ::date 2012-11-18...
# ::snt "Even flowers that have thorns ?"
# ::save-date Thu Oct 29, 2015 ...
(f / flower :mode interrogative
   :mod (e / even)
   :ARG0-of (h / have-03
      :ARG1 (t / thorn)))
```

Figure 3: Example of two sentences (slightly truncated for place reasons) in an AMR file (taken from *The Little Prince* corpus, available at the AMR project website)

Nearly all available annotated AMR corpora use the PENMAN graph serialisation format (Kaspar, 1989; shown in figure 1 together with a graphical representation where instances and concepts are shown in one rectangle for better readability, the full visualisation of figure 1 would be the visualisation in figure 2).

In addition to the PENMAN serialisation, typical AMR files contain some metadata too: the sentence itself, translations, a unique sentence identification, annotator identification, saving date, named entities, etc, e.g., figure 3.

Since the AMR graph is not anchored, i.e., there is no obvious link between words of the sentences and concepts, instances and relations in the graph, annotation of a corpus using a simple text editor is not possible. Apart from the parentheses it would be very difficult to check manually whether the concepts are correctly chosen and the arguments (notably `:ARG0` to `:ARG9`) defined for the chose concepts. The corpora mentioned in the AMR project website have mostly been annotated and validated using the AMR editor (Hermjakob, 2013) at https://amr.isi.edu/editor.html. Since this tool is not available for download, and we wanted to annotate a specialised evaluation corpus, we started developping metAMoRphosED. Our aim was a utility easy to use for annotators without any profound knowledge of semantic graphs, PENMAN format or triplets and providing as much assistance to the annotators as possible.

2 Architecture

metAMoRphosED is a webserver (implemented in python), the graphical user interface (GUI; implemented using html, css and javascript) is accessible with an internet browser. The server will handle the AMR file and optionally additional validation information like PropBank-data, a list of valid relations or a file which defines the relations an instance of which concepts can have. Start the server with

```
server.py --file amr-file.txt \
     --pbframes propbank-frames/frames \
     --reification reification-table.txt \
     --relations amr-relation-list.txt \
     --concepts amr-concept-list.txt \
     --constraints constraints.yml
```

and point your internet browser to `http://localhost:4567`. Once you have clicked on `load sentence`, a view similar to the one in figure 4 appears. In addition to the sentence, the PENMAN serialisation and the visualisation, the graphical user interface shows the PropBank documentation of all the verbs found in the graph, and possible errors.

2.1 Graph validation

In order to help the annotators metAMoRphosED can load AMR-related data to find potential annotation errors. metAMoRphosED will not modify a graph on its own without user approval, but it will issue warnings.

- concept definitions: since metAMoRphosED has been primarily developed to edit AMR graphs, it can load PropBank data to validate `:ARGn` relations of verbal concepts. In order to do so the option `--pbframes <propbank frames directory>` can be used

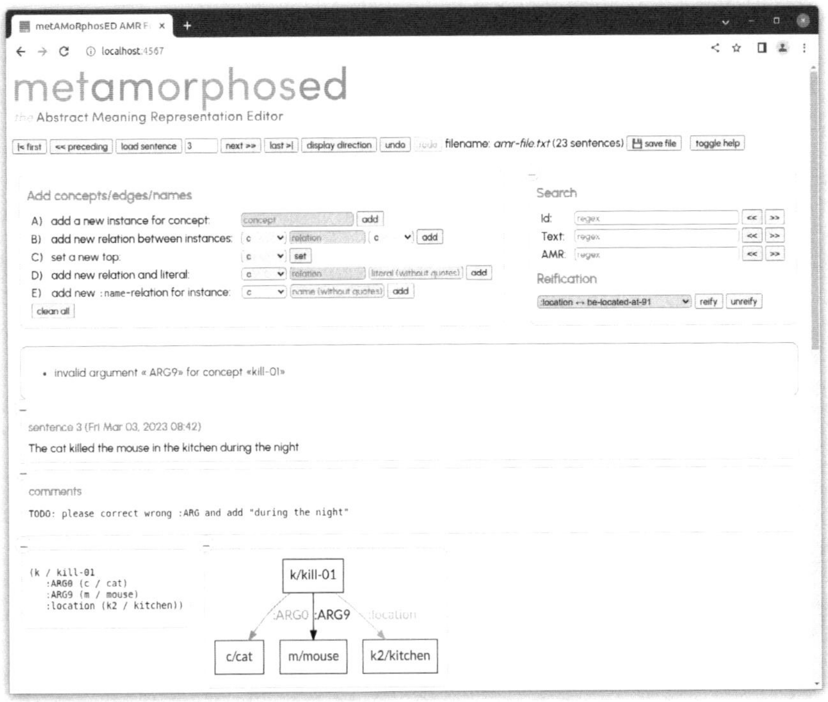

Figure 4: Initial screen with a sentence loaded, comments and an error message

to point to the `frames/` directory PropBank (available at https://github.com/propbank/propbank-frames). In addition to validation, metAMoRphosED will show all senses of all verbal concepts in the current graph (cf. figure 5).

- valid relations: the option `--relations <filename>` accepts a simple text file which contains a list of all valid relations (including inverted `-of` relations. If a graph contains a relation not in the list, a warning is given. Duplicated relations between two instances (e.g., two `:ARG0` relations) are also indicated as an error.

  The editor verifies that instances with outgoing `:opn` or `:sntn` relations, metAMoRphosED have a correct sequence of `:op1` to `:opn` without any missing number.

- relation constraints: a more specific way of limiting the possible range values of relations comes with the option `--constraints <constraints.yml>`, for instance:

```
# constraints for domain/relation/range
subjects:
# name-instances can only have :opn relations,
# which in turn have quoted strings as ranges
# (an initial _ indicates that the predicate
# or object is a regex)
name:
  _:op\d:
    - _".*"

# date-entity instances must only have
# :month, :day and :year predicates with
# integer values or :dayperiod with any value
date-entity:
  :month:
    - _[01]\d?
  :day:
    - _[0-3]\d?
  :year:
    - _\d\d\d\d
  :dayperiod:
```

- reification: the AMR documentation lists a set of relations which can be reified, metAMoRphosED proposes a function for this (cf. figure 6), which can be activated using the option `--reifications <table>`[3].

2.2 Non-AMR data

metAMoRphosED is not confined to AMR-data only. As long as the data to be edited can be represented

[3]See https://github.com/amrisi/amr-guidelines/blob/master/amr.md for more details on reification in AMR.

Figure 5: PropBank documentation (clipped)

Figure 6: search and reification/dereification

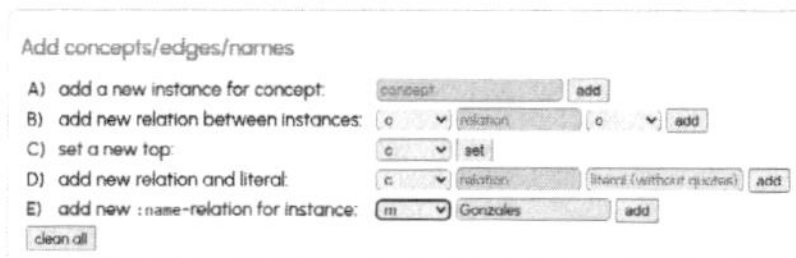

Figure 7: add menu

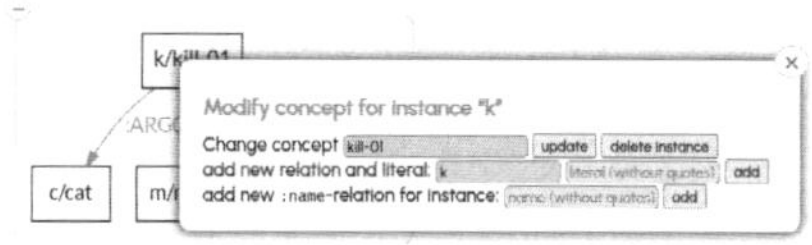

Figure 8: modify a concept

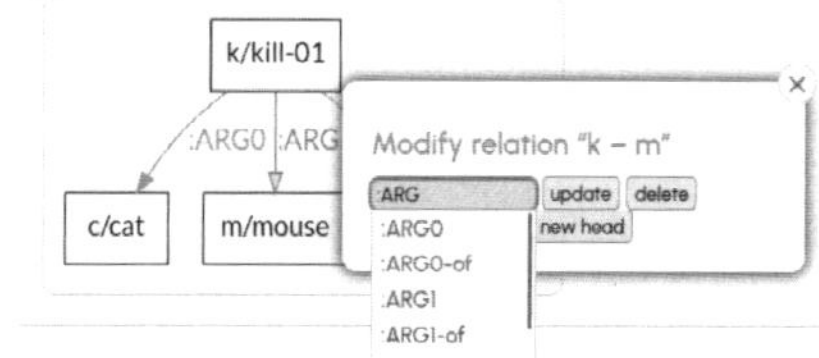

Figure 9: modify a relation

using the PENMAN format the tool is able to process it. I.e. the data must contain concepts, instances, attributes (literals) and directed relations between them. This means that pure RDF (in contrast to RDFS) can not be annotated, neither can data taken from wikidata be edited directly due to the qualifiers, i.e. triples with an property in subject position.

However data like the MultiWOZ corpus can be transformed into PENMAN and than be edited by metAMoRphosED (Abrougui et al., 2023).

3 Editing functions

metAMoRphosED can create new graphs from scratch (in this case, the AMR-file must contain at least `()`) or can be used to modify existing graphs (possibly generated by an AMR parser). Apart from graphical operations a direct modification of the PENMEN serialisation is possible. After every modification the current version of the graph is visualised. Navigation within the current file is possible by giving the sentence number, navigation buttons (first, last, next, preceding) or search functions (sentence id, sentence text, PENMAN, cf. figure 6) with highlighted results.

In order to add new instances or literals and new relations between new and existing instances, an input form is provided in the GUI (figure 7). Existing data can be modified or deleted by clicking on instances or relations in the graph visualisation (cf. figures 8 and 9). In case of an unwanted modification an *undo* function exists to revert the graph to the preceding version.

In AMR the entry point of a graph contains topic information, in order to change the entry point a *set top* function is provided.

As mentioned above, if metAMoRphosED was started with the option `--reification`, all relations listed correctly in the loaded reification table can be automatically reified (and unreified if no additional relation exists). So for instance the graph shown in figure 4 is transformed into the graph of figure 10.

If the loaded AMR file is under git version control, clicking the save file button also performs a `git add`/`git commit`.

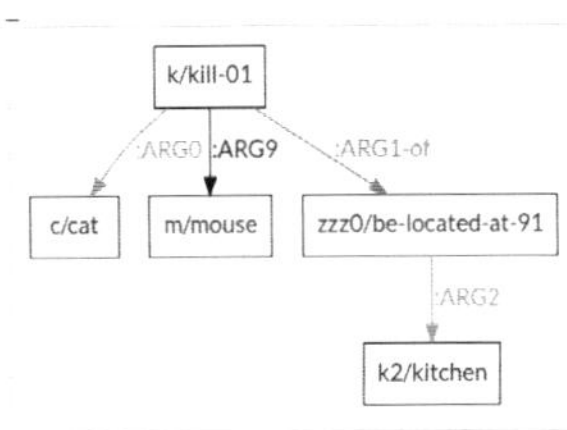

Figure 10: relation `:location` reified

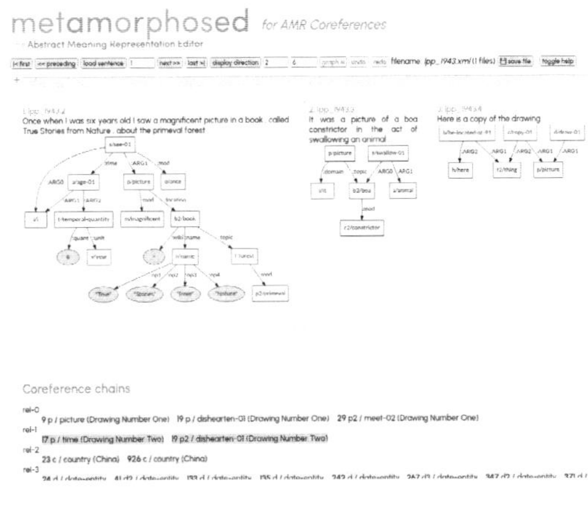

Figure 11: AMR coreference editor interface (clipped)

4 Comparison

Since the existing AMR editor (Hermjakob, 2013) is not available for download, we were not able to compare the anotation speed and ergonomics of metAMoRphosED and ISI's editor. Since AMR data is stored in PENMAN format, some might find it more difficult to "understand" than a graphical representation. In general, annotation speed depends mainly of the competence and experience of the annotators and much less on the tool. However the graphical representaion which metAMoRphosED proposes, makes it easier for annotators new to AMR.

5 Conclusion and prospectives

We presented a novel graph editor, suitable to create or modify and validate Abstract Meaning Representation graphs in a visual mode. All modifications are git-version controlable. The code is actively maintained and available at https://github.com/Orange-Opensource/metamorphosed. metAMoRphosED is currently used to annotate a test corpus containing 400 questions and turned out to be stable.

Apart from an interface to annotate AMR coreferences, which has been implemented and is being tested (cf. figure 11) we plan several future developments, notably a multi-user system, where multiple users can annotate the same file with integrated calculation of annotator agreement. Another improvement could be an automatic search of similar sentences in a reference corpus (such as AMR 3.0) to ensure that similar constructions and sentences are annotated homogenously. Other ideas include providing a way to integrate plugins which could run queries to external systems to facilitate the annotation as much as possible. We will consider comments and issues posted by users to decide which feature is the most urgent to be implemented first.

Acknowledgments

We'd like to thank the anonymous reviewers for comments and ideas to improve this paper.

References

Rim Abrougui, Géraldine Damnati, Johannes Heinecke, and Frédéric Béchet. 2023. Abstract Representation for Multi-Intent Spoken Language Understanding. In *International Conference on Acoustics, Speech, and Signal Processing*, Rhodes Island, Greece. IEEE.

Laura Banarescu, Claire Bonial, Shu Cai, Madalina Georgescu, Kira Griffitt, Ulf Hermjakob, Kevin Knight, Philipp Koehn, Martha Palmer, and Nathan Schneider. 2013. Abstract Meaning Representation for Sembanking. In *Proceedings of the 7th Linguistic Annotation Workshop and Interoperability with Discourse*, pages 178–186, Sofia, Bulgaria. Association for Computational Linguistics.

Rexhina Blloshmi, Rocco Tripodi, and Roberto Navigli. 2020. XL-AMR: Enabling Cross-Lingual AMR Parsing with Transfer Learning Techniques. In *Proceedings of the 2020 Conference on Empirical Methods in Natural Language Processing (EMNLP)*, page 2487–2500, Online. Association for Computational Linguistics.

Marco Damonte and Shay B. Cohen. 2018. Cross-lingual Abstract Meaning Representation Parsing. In *Annual Conference of the North American Chapter of the Association for Computational Linguistics: Human Language Technologies*, pages 1146–1155, New Orleans, Lousiana, USA. Association for Computational Linguistics.

Johannes Heinecke and Anastasia Shimorina. 2022. Multilingual Abstract Meaning Representation for Celtic Languages. In *Proceedings of the 4th Celtic Language Technology Workshop within LREC2022*, pages 1–6, Marseille. ELRA.

Ulf Hermjakob. 2013. AMR Editor: A Tool to Build Abstract Meaning Representations. https://amr.isi.edu/papers/amr-editor-ulf2013a.pdf.

Hans Kamp and Uwe Reyle. 1993. *From Discourse to Logic. Introduction to Modeltheoretic Semantics of Natural Language, Formal Logic and Discourse Representation Theory*. Studies in Linguistics and Philosophy 42. Kluwer, Dordrecht.

Robert T. Kaspar. 1989. A Flexible Interface for Linking Applications to Penman's Sentence Generator. In *Proceedings of the Workshop on Speech and Natural Language*, pages 153–158, Philadelphia, PA. Association for Computational Linguistics.

Paul Kingsbury and Martha Palmer. 2002. From Tree-Bank to PropBank. In *Proceedings of the Third International Conference on Language Resources and Evaluation*, Las Palmas, Canary Islands - Spain. European Language Resources Association.

Martha Palmer, Daniel Gildea, and Paul Kingsbury. 2005. The Proposition Bank: An Annotated Corpus of Semantic Roles. *Computational Linguistics*, 31(1):71–106.

Sarah Uhrig, Yoalli Rezepka García, Juri Opits, and Anette Frank. 2021. Translate, then Parse! A strong baseline for Cross-Lingual AMR Parsing. In *Proceedings of the 17th International Conference on Parsing Technologies and the IWPT 2021 Shared Task on Parsing into Enhanced Universal Dependencies*, pages 58–64, Online. Association for Computational Linguistics.

Personal Noun Detection for German

Carla Sökefeld
Universität Hamburg
carla.soekefeld@uni-hamburg.de

Melanie Andresen
University of Stuttgart
melanie.andresen@uni-stuttgart.de

Johanna Binnewitt
Bundesinstitut für Berufsbildung
Johanna.Binnewitt@bibb.de

Heike Zinsmeister
Universität Hamburg
heike.zinsmeister@uni-hamburg.de

Abstract

Common nouns denoting human beings such as *teacher* or *visitor*—henceforth **personal nouns**—play an important role in manifesting gender and gender stereotypes in texts, especially for languages with grammatical gender like German. Automatically detecting and extracting personal nouns can thus be of interest for a wide range of different tasks such as minimizing gender bias in language models and researching gender stereotypes or gender-fair language. However, personal noun detection is complicated by the morphological heterogeneity and ambiguity of personal and non-personal nouns, which restrict lexicon-based approaches. In this paper, we introduce the new task of personal noun detection and present a classifier that detects personal nouns in German, created by fine-tuning a BERT-based transformer model. Although some phenomena like ambiguity and metalinguistic uses are still problematic, the model is able to classify personal nouns with robust performance (f1-score: 0.94).

1 Motivation

Following Elmiger (2018), personal nouns are common nouns denoting humans such as kinship terms (*daughter*) or occupational titles (*teacher*). They form a segment of the animacy hierarchy (Silverstein, 1976), which is widely used in language typology, see Figure 1. Personal nouns correspond to the segment characterized as [–proper, +human], between proper names and common nouns denoting non-human living beings.

Identifying personal nouns is not only motivated by typological interests. In German, a language with a tri-partite grammatical gender system (masculine, feminine, neuter), there are morphological means to express the gender of the persons referred to, which leads to a congruent interpretation of grammatical form and human gender (such as *mother* and *father* or *actor* and *actress* in English). In recent years, there has been a vigorous debate in Germany whether to consequently disambiguate personal nouns in concordance with the gender of their referents (Kunkel-Razum, 2020). The actual implementation in texts varies between using masculine forms as the traditional 'general' expression (e.g. *die Zuschauer* ['the spectators, masculine']), explicit markings of feminized (e.g. *die Zuschauerinnen* ['the spectators, feminine']) and gender-diverse forms with a special character and feminine suffix (e.g. *die Zuschauer:innen* ['the spectators, gender-diverse']), or using neutral forms (e.g. *die Zuschauenden* ['the spectators, neutralized for gender']).

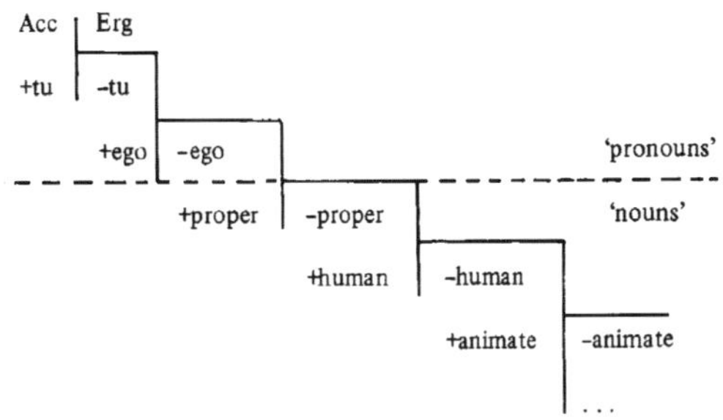

Figure 1: Personal nouns form the segment [–proper, +human]. The animacy hierarchy of Silverstein (1976) was originally introduced for typological analyses of 'accusative' vs. 'ergative' case-marking splits.

As a result, personal nouns are a crucial part of expressing gender in German texts, and thus also a crucial part of manifesting gender stereotypes in texts. The detection of personal nouns is useful for analyzing these stereotypes from various perspectives.

Gender bias in large language models or their training data has become an active research field

Proceedings of the 19th Joint ACL - ISO Workshop on Interoperable Semantic Annotation, pages 33–39
June 20, 2023. ©2023 Association for Computational Linguistics

in NLP.[1] There are methods of detecting gender bias in word embeddings such as the Word Embedding Association Test (WEAT) (Caliskan et al., 2017). One method of balancing gender in the training data, for example, is 'Counterfactual Data Augmentation' (Lu et al., 2019) which is based on adding synthetic sentences to the training corpus that are created by means of a bidirectional lexicon of gendered words such as *actor:actress*. In languages like German, such a lexicon would need to include all personal nouns, because German uses lexical and morphological means very productively to create their feminized or neuter forms.

From a linguistic standpoint, recent developments of gender-fair language in German (Kunkel-Razum, 2020) have led to increasing interest in the forms and use of personal nouns, e.g. regarding frequencies of feminized forms (*Student* ['student, masculine'] > *Studentin* ['student, feminine']) or neutral forms derived from a verbal participle form (*Studenten* ['students, masculine'] > *Studierende* ['people who study, plural, neutralized for gender']). Newer overtly gender-inclusive forms employ e.g. an asterisk (*Wähler*innen* ['voters, female plural suffix']) or a colon (*Bürger:innen* ['citizens, female plural suffix']) to explicitly include not only women but people of all non-binary genders. The problem with researching these phenomena in a quantitative way is that it has not been possible to gauge the basic population of personal nouns in a given corpus in order to put frequencies of e.g. forms with an asterisk into perspective, for instance to approximate whether such forms are getting more frequent.

This is due to personal nouns being a heterogeneous class in German that includes the products of many different word formation processes. Derivational suffixes for personal nouns, for example, include *-er* (*Lehrer* 'teacher'), *-ung* (*Leitung* 'leader/manager') and *-ling* (*Lehrling* 'apprentice'). This heterogeneity is further complicated by some personal nouns being ambiguous with non-personal nouns, e.g. *Leitung* 'leader, manager' vs. *Leitung* 'wire, pipeline', restricting the use of word-list based approaches like Kokkinakis et al. (2015) for Swedish vocational terms. Furthermore, other nouns that do not refer to a human contain these suffixes as well (e.g. *Gräber* 'graves', *Fälschung* 'forgery', *Frischling* 'shoat'), leading to false positives when querying a corpus for these word formation patterns. Thus, it is not possible to identify all personal nouns in a corpus with a regular expression without extensive manual correction. Instead, machine learning-based token classification could be the way to go.

To test the feasibility of such a semantic annotation, we have fine-tuned a pre-trained language model on manually annotated data to automatically identify personal nouns in a corpus. We discuss problems of the annotation and perform a qualitative error analysis on the results. The classifier model is freely available.[2]

While our work focuses on German, research on gender-fair language has been conducted for other gendered languages as well (see Robiche 2018 for French and Verelst 2022 for Dutch). Thus, a classifier that is able to detect personal nouns could also be fruitful for research in other languages.

2 Previous work on personal nouns

Quantitative work on personal nouns in German so far has either looked at pre-chosen lexemes where it is possible to extract all forms of the whole paradigm and thus know the basic population (e.g. Elmiger et al. 2017; Adler and Plewnia 2019), or has resorted to manually identify personal nouns in a corpus (e.g. Ivanov et al. 2018, Acke 2019, Müller-Spitzer et al. 2022). Elmiger (2018, 184) defines personal nouns as "nominal expressions that are used [...] to refer to human beings". While this definition might seem straightforward, it is often difficult to determine if a noun is indeed used to refer to human beings. Some problems identified in Elmiger et al. (2017) include ambiguous nouns and collective nouns that can be used either in a personalized way (1-a) or instead referring to an institution or organization (1-b) (Elmiger et al., 2017, 195-197) .

(1) a. Most Democrats voted in favor of the motion.
    b. The Democrats lost votes to the Republicans.

These issues, especially ambiguity, lead to the problem that even to query specific lexemes in a corpus will yield false positives, for example for nouns such as *Berliner* that can be used both as an adjec-

[1] See, e.g., the workshop series on Gender Bias in Natural Language Processing (https://genderbiasnlp.talp.cat/) and their proceedings on https://aclanthology.org/.

[2] https://huggingface.co/CarlaSoe/personal-noun-detection-german-bert.

tive and as a noun, and which has a personal and non-personal meaning as a noun on top of that, see the examples in (2).

(2) a. Er ist ein *Berliner* Bäcker.
'He is a *Berlin* baker'
"He is a baker from *Berlin*."
b. Er ist ein *Berliner*.
"He is a *Berliner*." (Berlin native)
c. Er isst einen *Berliner*.
"He eats a *donut*."

While POS annotation can help to distinguish the adjectival from the nominal use, it does not help to distinguish between the latter two nominal usages.

In the context of digital humanities, Flüh and Schumacher (2021) trained a classifier to extract and assign gender roles in German literary texts, targeting personal nouns as well as proper names of literary characters. While the task of automatically detecting personal nouns is similar to Named-Entity Recognition as it is a token classification task, it differs insofar as the tokens to be detected are crucially not named entities—proper names are not part of the semantic class of personal nouns.

3 The personal noun detection task

Objective. The objective of the detection task is a binary classification of all tokens in a corpus as either personal noun (PERS_N) or other (O).

Conceptually, a personal noun is a token *t* in a text that meets the following criteria: (i) the lexical-semantic class of *t* is [–proper, +human]; (ii) *t* is used in a context that refers to a person or a group of humans; (iii) the part of speech of *t* is common noun.

Following Elmiger's (2018) approach to personal nouns, the detection task targets all noun tokens denoting humans regardless of their referential context, including generic, non-generic, and predicative contexts. Metonymic uses of nouns—such as referring to an institution or an organization instead of referring to a person—are labeled "other" (O) according to criterion (ii). For example, *Gewinnerin* ('winner, female') in example (3), which refers to the Green Party, is labeled O.

(3) [...] die Grüne Partei der Schweiz (GPS) [ist] die große *Gewinnerin* [...]
"[...] the Green Party of Switzerland (GPS) [is] the big *winner* [...]"

Furthermore, the task excludes personal noun instances that occur as the first part of a compound noun such as *Bauern* in example (4).[3] Because the token *Bauern-Proteste* refers to the event of 'protest', and only the subtoken *Bauern* fulfills the definition of a personal noun, it is disregarded for the annotation.

(4) Die größten *Bauern*-Proteste gab es in Bonn.
"The biggest *farmers*' protests took place in Bonn."

Proper names are, by definition, not personal nouns and are labeled "other" (O).

We would like to point out that the task operates on the token level, instead of the phrasal level, because our research interest are forms of gender-fair language in German. This is essentially expressed on the lexical level even if it requires contextual and referential disambiguation. The personal noun detection task is therefore different from, e.g., the task of (phrasal) markable detection in coreference resolution.

3.1 Data

We use the corpus from Sökefeld (2021) which consists of roughly 130,000 tokens from two different text types (newspaper and blog). The news subcorpus was compiled by selecting twelve articles each from the politics section of seven German online news outlets.[4] For the blog subcorpus, posts from the blogging platform `wordpress.com` were selected that had been tagged either as "Alltag" ('everyday life') or as "Tagebuch" ('diary') in order to capture more colloquial language use.

For the new task of personal noun detection, we enriched the corpus with additional annotations (see section 3.2).

Because of copyright issues, it is not possible to share the corpus, but metadata with links to the articles and blog posts is provided with the classifier model (see Section 3.3).

3.2 Annotation

In the initial corpus, only personal nouns that refer to a person or people of more than one gender as in

[3] Compounding is very productive in German and results either in merged words without a space or in hyphenated compounds.

[4] *Bild*, *Frankfurter Rundschau*, *Neues Deutschland*, *Süddeutsche Zeitung*, *taz. die tageszeitung*, *Die Welt*, and *Die Zeit*.

Data	Tokens	Types
Training	3,342	1,331
Test	384	289

Table 1: PERS_N types and tokens in training and test set.

example (5)[5], or where the gender of the referent(s) is unclear as in example (6), had been annotated manually.

(5) Die meisten *Migranten* zogen weg, nur fünf Familien blieben.
"Most *migrants* moved away, only five families stayed."

(6) Am besten holt ihr noch ein Familienmitglied oder eine/n gute/n *Freund/in* ins Boot.
"It would be best if you got a family member or a good *friend* on board."

For the personal noun detection task, the original corpus was enriched and all personal nouns with a gender-specific referent (either a male or female individual, or a group of only male or female people) were annotated with a semi-automatic approach. This was conducted in four steps: First, a list of word forms was derived from Sökefeld's (2021) annotations; Second, the list was applied to automatically tag all additional gender-specific instances of these word forms in the corpus; Third, the resulting annotations were manually corrected and, fourth, additional personal noun tokens that had not been included in the earlier list of word forms were annotated in the correction process. The second step yielded many false-positive labels for ambiguous word forms such as *Deutsche* 'German', which can either be used as a personal noun or as an adjective, or *Alter* 'old person'; 'age', suggesting that an approach of matching a list of previously discerned personal nouns to a corpus would not yield sufficient accuracy. All manual annotation was carried out by one annotator.

All in all, the label PERS_N was not very prevalent in the data. There were only 3,726 tokens (roughly 3%, 1,441 different types) labeled as PERS_N compared to 126,459 "other" tokens.

3.3 Training

We split the sentence-wise annotated corpus in 10% test data and 90% training data for fine-tuning a token classifier[6] based on the pre-trained language model *bert-base-german-cased*[7] for the new task of personal noun detection.

Since the personal noun annotation was performed on the token level, we applied the transformer tokenizer on already tokenized sentences. We used the default hyperparameters for training[8] and evaluated the model on token level on the remaining 10% of the corpus (with 384 tokens (289 types) marked as PERS_N). Of the personal nouns in the test set, 110 types were out-of-vocabulary in the sense of not being present in the training set (although they might be present in the pre-trained language model). Table 1 shows the distribution of personal noun types and tokens in the training and test set.

The fine-tuned model and information on the corpus (metadata and URLs to the original texts) are provided on Huggingface.[9]

Label	Precision	Recall	f1-Score	Support
O	1.00	1.00	1.00	12,495
PERS_N	0.94	0.93	0.94	384
PERS_N$_{OOV}$	1.00	0.88	0.93	113

Table 2: Results of the fine-tuned model on the test set, with scores for overall PERS_N-types and OOV-PERS_N-types.

4 Results and discussion

The results of the fine-tuned model's performance on the test data are shown in Table 2. The results were quite good for both recall and precision, particularly considering the small amount of data and the low frequency of the target category in this data. Performance on out-of-vocabulary types (see Section 3.3) was similar to the overall results, but with a higher precision and a lower recall.

Overall, there were 22 cases of false positives (see (7) for an example) and 27 cases of false negatives (see (8) for an example) in the test data. Ex-

[5]Target words are italicized in the examples.

[6]By following the tutorial on `https://huggingface.co/course/chapter7/2?fw=pt` (last used May 8th 2023).

[7]`https://huggingface.co/bert-base-german-cased` (last used May 8th 2023)

[8]As specified in the huggingface tutorial, see footnote 6: Number of training epochs: 3; learning rate: $2e^{-5}$; weight decay: 0.01.

[9]`https://huggingface.co/CarlaSoe/personal-noun-detection-german-bert/tree/main`.

ample (7) showcases an interesting example of a false positive that could be considered a peripheral, non-prototypical personal noun, as a generation is made up of people. The model's classification of this token showcases that some categorization decisions are not as clear-cut as they may seem on the surface.

(7) Von Generation zu *Generation* schwand das Wissen um den Ursprung des Wohlstands der Familie.
"The knowledge about the origin of the family's wealth faded from generation to *generation*."

(8) Du bist ein elender *Heuchler*.
"You are a wretched *hypocrite*."

The personal noun *Heuchler* in example (8) was not detected by the model as such. This could be due to its relative infrequency.[10] It was also not part of the training data for the fine-tuning.

On closer inspection, though, the false negatives and positives in some cases revealed not a mistake of the model, but an error in the manual annotation. These included errors from the automatic annotation that were not caught and corrected during the manual correction, such as *Deutschen* being categorized as a personal noun in example (9). These oversights stress the importance of using more than one annotator when manually labeling data, so that errors like this can be avoided.

(9) Ähnlich äußerte sich der Präsident des *Deutschen* Städtetags [...]
"The president of the *German* Association of Cities expressed himself similarly [...]"

Apart from looking at the model's performance on the test data, we also tested instances of challenging phenomena as identified by Elmiger (2018) that make distinguishing between personal nouns and other words difficult.

First of all, ambiguity can pose a problem. We tested the two word forms *Berliner* and *Hamburger* that can both be used as an adjective and as a noun, as well as having both a personal noun usage and a 'food' meaning. Both word forms were correctly not classified as a personal noun in their adjectival usage, but *Berliner* as a noun was labeled a personal noun in both the 'food' usage and the 'person from Berlin' usage. For *Hamburger*, on the other hand, the model correctly only labeled the usage as a personal noun as such.

Secondly, personalized and institutional usages of collective nouns were tested with the word forms *Polizei* 'police' and *Menge* 'amount', 'crowd'. For both word forms, the model managed to correctly label the personalized usage as a personal noun in example (10-a), and not label the impersonal usage in example (10-b).

(10) a. Die *Polizei* schoss auf Demonstrant:innen.
"The *police* shot at protestors."
b. Die *Polizei* ist Teil der Exekutive.
"The *police* is part of the executive."

Proper names could also pose a problem for the classification, as a lot of last names are derived from personal nouns but should not be detected by the model. In fact, the model was able to differentiate correctly between personal noun, in example (11-a), and proper name usage, in example (11-b), for *Schneider* ('tailor'), but it did not detect *Müller* ('miller') as a personal noun in example (11-c), which is the most common family name in Germany,[11] but the occupation has become rare, so that *Müller* only appears as a last name in the training data and not in its personal noun usage.

(11) a. Ich bringe ein Hemd zum *Schneider*.
"I bring a shirt to the *tailor*."
b. Frau *Schneider* sitzt auf einer Bank.
"Ms *Schneider* is sitting on a bench."
c. Ich bringe das Getreide zum *Müller*.
"I bring the grain to the *miller*."

Finally, we tested how the model responds to metalinguistic uses of personal nouns. The model labeled the word forms of *Frau* and *Mann* in their metalinguistic uses in the examples in (12) as personal nouns.

(12) a. *Frauen* ist der Plural von *Frau*.
"*Women* is the plural of *woman*."
b. Das Wort *Mann* ist ein Nomen.
"The word *man* is a noun."

(13) "*Frauen*" ist der Plural von "*Frau*".
"'*Women*' is the plural of '*woman*'."

[10]See `https://corpora.uni-leipzig.de/de/res?corpusId=deu_news_2022&word=Heuchler` (last used May 8th 2023) for frequency information.

[11]For a list of common family names in Germany see `https://de.wiktionary.org/wiki/Verzeichnis:Deutsch/Namen/die_hufigsten_Nachnamen_Deutschlands` (last used May 8th 2023)

Interestingly, when adding quotation marks to the sentence in (12-a) as in example (13), the model only labeled *Frau* as a personal noun, but not *Frauen*. For the sentence in example (12-b), though, it did not make a difference whether *Mann* was set in quotation marks or not.

Another challenge for the study of gender-fair language is that new forms keep evolving. Testing the new colon form (e.g. *Schüler:innen* 'students') that became popular only after the training corpus was compiled in 2019, the model still labeled the token *Demonstrant:innen* in example (14) as a personal noun. This shows that it could be useful for identifying new strategies of gender-fair language emerging in the future as well.

(14) Die Polizei schoss auf *Demonstrant:innen*.
"The police shot at *protestors*."

5 Conclusion

Personal nouns, the semantic class of common nouns denoting humans, are of great importance in the context of current discussions and developments in research on gender-fair language and language use in linguistics and digital humanities, as well as gender-fair NLP. In order to facilitate quantitative research, we defined the task of personal noun detection and fine-tuned a pre-trained language model for the detection of personal nouns in German.

The fine-tuning yielded surprisingly good results (f1-score: 0.94), considering the small amount of training data and the fact that the actual tokens of interest were not very prevalent. Further training on more diverse data including other text types, for example literary texts, which probably contain a range of different personal nouns not covered in news writing or personal blog posts, could improve the results even more. New training data could also include specifically selected sentences containing some of the more difficult to distinguish words as discussed in Section 4, like ambiguous words, proper names, and metalinguistic usages.

So far, the classifier only detects personal nouns but does not give any additional information on them. Ideally, a future version of the model would further enrich this classification. An initial expansion could be to detect grammatical gender. Much less trivial, but desirable, would be to implement a further classification of the type of reference, as qualitative research has shown that gender-fair forms tend to be used more frequently in cases of non-generic reference (Pettersson 2011, Sökefeld 2021). Incorporating a distinction between generic (15) and non-generic (16) use (see Friedrich and Pinkal 2015) into the classifier would make it possible to test whether this holds true on a larger scale.

(15) Kein *Bauarbeiter* hält bis 69 durch.
"No *construction worker* will manage to keep it up until the age of 69."

(16) Als Reaktion sprangen *Schüler*innen* und *Studierende* zunächst über die Drehkreuze an den Zugängen zu den Bahnsteigen.
"As a reaction, *pupils* and *students* initially jumped the barriers at the entry to the platform."

Similarly, whether a personal noun refers gender-specifically (e.g. masculine *Lehrer* referring to only male teachers) or gender-independently (e.g. masculine *Lehrer* referring to a mixed-gender group of teachers) is necessary information in order to quantify the amount of masculine personal nouns used to refer to gender-diverse groups.

Training the language model to classify personal nouns in these three categories would thus be a next step.

6 Ethics statement

We are aware that the corpus we used as training data contains texts that potentially include gender stereotypes. A possible application of our classifier could be to identify such stereotypical depictions.

References

Hanna Acke. 2019. Sprachwandel durch feministische Sprachkritik: Geschlechtergerechter Sprachgebrauch an den Berliner Universitäten. *Zeitschrift für Literaturwissenschaft und Linguistik*, 49(2):303–320.

Astrid Adler and Albrecht Plewnia. 2019. Die Macht der großen Zahlen. Aktuelle Spracheinstellungen in Deutschland. In Ludwig M. Eichinger, editor, *Neues vom Heutigen Deutsch: Empirisch - Methodisch - Theoretisch*, in Jahrbuch des Instituts für Deutsche Sprache. De Gruyter, Boston, MA.

Aylin Caliskan, Joanna J Bryson, and Arvind Narayanan. 2017. Semantics derived automatically from language corpora contain human-like biases. *Science*, 356(6334):183–186.

Daniel Elmiger. 2018. French anthroponyms as a heterogeneous category: Is there such a thing as personal nouns? *International Journal of Language and Culture*, 5(2):184–202.

Daniel Elmiger, Eva Schaeffer-Lacroix, and Verena Tunger. 2017. Geschlechtergerechte Sprache in Schweizer Behördentexten. Möglichkeiten und Grenzen einer mehrsprachigen Umsetzung. In Constanze Spieß and Martin Reisigl, editors, *Sprache und Geschlecht. Band 1: Sprachpolitiken und Grammatik*, volume 90 of *Osnabrücker Beiträge zur Sprachtheorie*, pages 61–90. Duisburg.

Marie Flüh and Mareike Schumacher. 2021. Digitale diachrone Korpusanalyse am Beispiel des Projekts "m*w – Gender Stereotype in der Literatur". In Gisela Mettele, Marint Prell, and Pia Marzell, editors, *Digital humanities and gender history*. Jena.

Annemarie Friedrich and Manfred Pinkal. 2015. Discourse-sensitive Automatic Identification of Generic Expressions. In *Proceedings of the 53rd Annual Meeting of the Association for Computational Linguistics and the 7th International Joint Conference on Natural Language Processing (Volume 1: Long Papers)*, pages 1272–1281, Beijing, China. Association for Computational Linguistics.

Christine Ivanov, Maria B. Lange, and Tabea Tiemeyer. 2018. Geschlechtergerechte Personenbezeichnungen in deutscher Wissenschaftssprache. Von frühen feministischen Vorschlägen für geschlechtergerechte Sprache zu deren Umsetzung in wissenschaftlichen Abstracts. *Suvremena lingvistika*, 44(86):261–290.

Dimitrios Kokkinakis, Ann Ighe, and Mats Malm. 2015. Gender-Based Vocation Identification in Swedish 19th Century Prose Fiction using Linguistic Patterns, NER and CRF Learning. In *Proceedings of the Fourth Workshop on Computational Linguistics for Literature*, pages 89–97, Denver, Colorado, USA. Association for Computational Linguistics.

Kathrin Kunkel-Razum. 2020. Gender-Neutral German: Asterisk or Underscore? *Germany #NOFilter*. Online. Goethe-Institut.

Kaiji Lu, Piotr Mardziel, Fangjing Wu, Preetam Amancharla, and Anupam Datta. 2019. Gender bias in neural natural language processing. *CoRR*, abs/1807.11714.

Carolin Müller-Spitzer, Jan Oliver Rüdiger, and Sascha Wolfer. 2022. Olaf Scholz gendert. Eine Analyse von Personenbezeichnungen in Weihnachts- und Neujahrsansprachen. *Linguistische Werkstattberichte*. Online.

Magnus Pettersson. 2011. *Geschlechtsübergreifende Personenbezeichnungen: eine Referenz- und Relevanzanalyse an Texten*. Vol. 11 in Europäische Studien zur Textlinguistik. Narr Verlag, Tübingen.

Lou Robiche. 2018. *Pratiques sociolinguistiques francophones de féminisation et de dégenrement*. Espaces discursifs. L'Harmattan, Paris.

Michael Silverstein. 1976. Hierarchy of features and ergativity. In R.M.W. Dixon, editor, *Grammatical categories in Australian languages*, pages 112–171. Australian Institute of Aboriginal Studies, Canberra. Re-published in: Pieter Muysken and Henk van Riemsdijk, editors, 1986. *Features and Projections*, pages 163–232. Foris, Dordrecht.

Carla Sökefeld. 2021. Gender(un)gerechte Personenbezeichnungen: derzeitiger Sprachgebrauch, Einflussfaktoren auf die Sprachwahl und diachrone Entwicklung. *Sprachwissenschaft*, 46(1):111–141.

Natalie Verelst. 2022. Movierung und generisches Maskulinum aus kontrastiver Perspektive. Talk presented at *Die Movierung. Formen – Funktionen – Bewertungen*, University of Passau.

ISO 24617-2 on a cusp of languages

Krzysztof Hwaszcz, Marcin Oleksy, Aleksandra Domogała, and **Jan Wieczorek**
Wrocław University of Science and Technology
{krzysztof.hwaszcz,marcin.oleksy,aleksandra.domogala, jan.wieczorek}@pwr.edu.pl

Abstract

The article discusses the challenges of cross-linguistic dialogue act annotation, which involves using methods developed for a multilingual framework to annotate conversations in a specific language. The article specifically focuses on the research on dialogue act annotation in Polish based on the ISO standard. To ensure applicability across languages, the standard was designed to be language-independent. The article examines the differences between Polish and English in dialogue act annotation based on selected examples from DiaBiz.Kom corpus, such as the use of honorifics in Polish, the use of inflection to convey meaning in Polish, the tendency to use complex sentence structures in Polish, and the cultural differences that may play a role in the annotation of dialogue acts. The article also discusses the creation of DiaBiz.Kom, a Polish dialogue corpus based on ISO 24617-2:2012[1] standard applied to 1100 transcripts.

1 Introduction: Setting the scene

The process of dialogue act annotation is useful for natural language understanding, speech recognition, and various other applications that require the analysis of spoken language. However, annotating dialogue acts in one language may not be sufficient for processing conversations in another language. In such cases, cross-lingual dialogue act annotation is required, which involves using methods developed for one language to annotate conversations in another language (Bunt et al., 2020; Petukhova et al., 2015).

The ISO 24167-2:2012 standard included native speakers of Belorussian, Dutch, English, French, German, Italian, Japanese, Korean, Romanian, and Swedish. Yet each language has its own specific instruments for expressing communicative functions (and qualifiers). That requires addressing various challenges, such as differences in grammar, syntax, and lexicon, which can affect the accuracy of the annotation process. This paper examines the research on dialogue act annotation in Polish based on ISO standard developed for a multilingual framework (Bunt et al., 2010a). Also, methods used to address these challenges are outlined.

2 Related works

On multiple occasions, when faced with challenges in annotating communication functions, we turned to the literature for inspiration, seeking ideas from existing solutions. For the theoretical background we refer to ISO/DIS 24617-2:2012 (Bunt et al., 2010b, 2012), which is based on particular innovations such as distinguishing between annotations and representations (according to the ISO Linguistic Annotation Framework (LAF, ISO 24612:2009) and sets of dialogue participants, dimensions, communicative functions, functional segments and qualifiers (inventory of DiAML). Both manual and automatic annotation of dialogue segments according to the ISO standard have been tested in practice and described (Keizer et al., 2011; Petukhova et al., 2014; Bunt et al., 2016; Chowdhury et al., 2016; Ngo et al., 2017; Gilmartin et al., 2018). The development of annotation standards for particular corpora can be vividly exemplified by the case of the Switchboard Dialogue Act Corpus (the collection of telephone conversations). The NXT-format Switchboard Corpus was created with additional annotations according to the international standard ISO 64217-2:2012 (Fang et al., 2012). The re-annotation shows the significance of both standard scheme improvement and combining different standards on the same linguistic material.

The DiaBiz.Kom corpus correlates with the DialogBank corpus – current gold annotation stan-

[1]We also consulted the second edition of the standard: ISO 24617-2:2019.

Proceedings of the 19th Joint ACL - ISO Workshop on Interoperable Semantic Annotation, pages 40–46
June 20, 2023. ©2023 Association for Computational Linguistics

dard. Most dialogues from the DialogBank corpus were taken from other corpora and re-segmented and re-annotated. All annotations were double-checked for inconsistencies, errors and omissions. The data include samples which may be considered illustrative examples for annotations (Bunt et al., 2016). Suggestions and remarks with regard to limitations and extensions of the ISO standard put forth by the authors of the DialogBank have subsequently been implemented in the updated versions of the ISO standard(Bunt et al., 2018)).

3 Polish dialogue corpus DiaBiz.Kom

The DiaBiz.Kom corpus development is an annotation effort performed simultaneously with the DiaBiz corpus creation. The DiaBiz (Pęzik et al., 2022) is a large, multimodal corpus of Polish telephone conversations conducted in varied business settings, comprising 3,766 call center interactions based on 110 business scripts. The recordings were then transcribed and enriched with punctuation. DiaBiz.Kom (Oleksy et al., 2022) was created as an annotation layer based on the ISO 24617-2:2012 standard applied to the 1100 transcripts derived from DiaBiz (10 dialogues for each dialogue script). Every dialogue is annotated by 3 persons: 2 independently working annotators and a super-annotator who resolves all annotation inconsistencies. The authors in the first place focused on communicative function and dimension annotation, then the functional and dependence relations were annotated. Currently, the corpus consists of 1 277 965 tokens (151 520 final annotations for communicative functions). The corpus sample is available under CC BY-NC-ND 4.0 license at: `http://hdl.handle.net/11321/886`.

4 Language differences in dialogue act annotation between Polish and English

Dialogue act annotation is the process of labeling utterances in a dialogue with a specific communicative function or speech act. While Polish and English share common dialogue act categories, such as "inform" and "question," their implementation may bear some noticeable differences between the two languages (Fang et al., 2012; Biały, 2016).

One difference is the use of honorifics in Polish. In Polish the use of formal or informal pronouns and verb forms depends on the relationship between the speakers, their social status, and the context of the conversation. Although the level of formality in the annotated dialogues between an agent and a client is rather consistent throughout and high, this aspect may still affect the annotation of dialogue acts such as "request", "instruct" or "apology," which may be expressed differently depending on the level of formality required.

Another difference is the use of inflection to convey meaning in Polish. Unlike English, which relies heavily on word order to convey meaning, Polish uses inflection to indicate the grammatical role of a word in a sentence. This can affect the annotation of dialogue acts such as "command," where the inflection of the verb may be more important than the word order.

Additionally, in Polish there is a greater tendency to use complex sentence structures[2], which can make it more challenging to identify and annotate dialogue acts accurately. In English, there is a preference for simpler sentence structures, which makes it easier to identify and annotate dialogue acts. Moreover, English has a more rigid word order in questions than Polish. In English, the standard word order for questions is to invert the subject and auxiliary verb and add a question word or particle at the beginning or end of the sentence (1). Polish, on the other hand, allows for more flexibility in word order in questions. While the standard Polish word order for questions is similar to that of English (2a), Polish also allows for alternative word orders depending on the emphasis or focus of the question: inverted word order without a question particle (2b) and inverted word order with the verb and object reversed (2c).

(1) Do you like pizza?

(2)
a. Czy lubisz pizzę?
b. Lubisz pizzę?
c. Pizzę lubisz?

Finally, cultural differences may also play a role in the annotation of dialogue acts in Polish and English. For example, in Polish culture the intended meaning may not be explicitly stated, but rather implied through context and cultural norms. This can make it more challenging to identify and annotate dialogue acts accurately in Polish. Also, similar communication behavior may take different forms. An example is the beginning of a conversation, in

[2]The assertion is based on the study conducted by Ostalak, who examined grammatical structures in sentences within formal topics (Ostalak, 2019). The author established that complex sentences in Polish constituted 26,23%, while these in English – 18,97%

which the interlocutors establish their positions in the conversation, for example, one of them shows willingness In English, it is typically an interaction:

"Can I help you?" [Offer] ↔ "Yes." [acceptOffer]

In contrast, in Polish it is usually a less elaborate, unidirectional structure. The expression of willingness to help is only in the form of a question. Essentially, it is an encouragement to the caller to state his or her problem right away. For this reason, we decided to label such segments as Interaction-Structuring.

5 Morphological richness in the language and its influence on annotations

Dialogue act annotation in morphologically rich languages, such as Polish, can be more challenging than in morphologically poor languages, such as English. This is because morphologically rich languages have a greater number of inflections and grammatical markers that can affect the interpretation of utterances. In morphologically rich languages the inflection of a word can change its meaning or grammatical function, which can have implications for the annotation of dialogue acts. For example, the use of a different verb form can indicate whether a request is polite or imperative. The use of case markers can also indicate the role of a noun in a sentence, which can affect the annotation of dialogue acts such as "offer" or "request."

Morphologically poor languages, such as English, have fewer inflections and grammatical markers, which can make it easier to identify and annotate dialogue acts. English relies more on word order and lexical cues to convey meaning, which makes it easier to identify the main clauses and subordinate clauses in a sentence.

However, morphologically poor languages like English also have their own challenges in dialogue act annotation. For example, English often uses indirect speech acts, where the intended meaning is not explicitly stated, but rather implied through context and cultural norms. This can make it more challenging to identify and annotate dialogue acts accurately in English. However, it is still possible to achieve accurate and reliable results with careful annotation guidelines and a thorough understanding of the language's grammar and syntax.

6 Multipolysemous words: Selected examples

Another issue that adds up to the challenges of dialogue act annotation in Polish is the notion of polysemous words. Such words have multiple meanings that can lead to ambiguity in their interpretation (Gruszczyńska et al., 2019; Lewandowska-Tomaszczyk and Thelen, 2013). When annotating dialogue acts, it is important to disambiguate the meaning of polysemous words to ensure that the intended dialogue act is accurately labeled (Silvano et al., 2022).

While annotating problematic examples, we were more likely to interpret words with identical orthographic form that have distinct meaning as different lexical units rather than as polysemous words. Thus, we were closer to a structural perspective (Apresjan, 1974; Bogusławski, 1976), than, for instance, a cognitive one (Lakoff, 2008). One challenge is identifying the context in which the polysemous word is used. Context plays a crucial role in disambiguating the meaning of a word (Mohammed, 2009; Schmidt, 2008). Therefore, it is important to consider the surrounding words and the larger context of the dialogue when annotating dialogue acts.

Annotators may also need to rely on their own personal (and subjective) knowledge and experience to disambiguate the meaning of polysemous words. This can be especially challenging when annotating dialogues that cover a wide range of topics.

Another challenge is to distinguish between the various meanings of a polysemous word. Some polysemous words may have meanings that are closely related, making it difficult to differentiate between them.

To mitigate these challenges, it is important to provide annotators with clear guidelines and instructions that specify how to disambiguate polysemous words. These guidelines should also include examples and explanations of how to interpret and annotate these words in different contexts. We have also developed substitution tests for selected cases. Additionally, it was helpful to have multiple iterations as well as annotator reviews and discuss the annotations to ensure consistency and accuracy in the labeling of dialogue acts.

Let us consider below a number of examples of polysemous words along with the approach we have adopted on the basis of annotator domain-specific knowledge and experience, tests as well as additional contextual information

6.1 "Proszę"

The most common translation of the Polish word "proszę" into English is "please". However, depending on the context and usage, it may also be translated as "thank you", "you're welcome", "excuse me" or "here you are". The range of possible translations inevitably triggers the number of functions it may take when annotating dialogue acts.

"Proszę" in Polish and "please" or "you're welcome" in English can be categorized as markers of politeness or as a response to a polite request or gratitude. In dialogue act annotation, the specific meaning of "proszę" would depend on the context and the speaker's intention. For instance, "proszę" in a phrase could be annotated as a Request (e.g., "Proszę mi pomóc", Eng. "Please help me."), or as an Accept Thanking in the dialogue turns like - "Dziękuję. - "Proszę bardzo." (Eng. - "Thank you" - "You're welcome"). In English, these two functions – namely Request and Accept Thanking would be split between two separate lexical items, the former function being reserved for "please", whilst the latter for "you're welcome".

All in all, we have distinguished five different dialogue functions (Accept Thanking - 19 cases, Accept Offer - 7, Contact Indication - 30, Contact Check - 1, Auto Negative - 1) for "proszę" illustrated in (3)-(7) below.

(3)

Agent: Dobrze. **Proszę**. [acceptThanking: SOM] "Agent: Alright. **You're welcome.**"

Klient: (...) Dobrze. **Dziękuję bardzo**. [thanking: SOM] "Client: (...) Good. Thank you very much."

(4)

Agent: Jasne. Tak, **mogę, mogę złożyć taką dyspozycję wyłączenia**. [Offer: Task] "Agent: Sure. Yes, I can, I can make such an exclusion order."

Klient: **Proszę**. [acceptOffer: Task] "Client: **Please**."

(5)

Klient: **Proszę**. [contactIndication: Contact Management/ opening: Discourse Structuring] "Client: **Hello**."

Agent: (yy) Dzień dobry. Czy ja dodzwoniłam się do pani..."Agent: (yy) Good morning. Have I reached Mrs...

(6)

Klient: (yy) siedemdziesiąt trzy, zero, osiem, zero, dwa. "Client: (yy) seventy-three, zero, eight, zero, two."

Agent: **Proszę... proszę...** [contactCheck: Contact Management] "Agent: **Go on... go on... / Yes... yes...**"

Klient: Zero, osiem... "Client: Zero, eight...

(7)

Klient: Tak, tak. "Client: Yes, yes."

Agent: To tak. "Agent: That's right."

Klient: **Proszę?** [autoNegative: Auto-Feedback] "Client: **Excuse me?**"

6.2 "Dobrze"

The word "dobrze" in Polish does not have its one English counterpart – the meaning lies on the verge of "okay" and "alright" (as expressions of agreement or acceptance), which makes it even more difficult to compare the two languages. In Polish "dobrze" can be used to indicate agreement, approval, or satisfaction, but it can also be used to indicate understanding or comprehension. In English, "okay" or "alright" are generally used to indicate agreement or acceptance, but – unlike in Polish – they may also be used to indicate indifference or lack of enthusiasm. The decision of the speaker to use "dobrze" in Polish can also depend on the social and cultural context of the conversation. For example, "dobrze" can be used to indicate politeness or deference to a speaker who is perceived to be of a higher social status. In English, "okay" or "alright" are generally used regardless of social context, but can be used to express politeness or informality depending on the situation. "Dobrze" in Polish can also imply a sense of satisfaction or contentment with the situation or outcome. It can also suggest a positive evaluation or endorsement of something. In English, "okay" or "alright" generally do not carry the same level of positive evaluation or endorsement. We have distinguished three different dialogue functions (Auto Positive - 3111 cases, Accept Request/Offer/Suggest - 400, Contact Indication - 12) for "dobrze" illustrated in (8)-(12) below.

(8)

Klient: Tak jest, dokładnie. Wróblewskiego szesnaście jest. "Client: Yes, exactly. It is Wróblewskiego sixteen."

Agent: **Dobrze.** [autoPositive: Auto-Feedback] "Agent: **Good.**

(9)

Agent: **Ale proszę się jeszcze tam skontaktować,** [Suggest: Task] (...)"Agent: **`But please still get in touch there,** (...)

Klient: **Dobrze.** [acceptSuggest: Task] Dziękuję. "Client: **Okay.** Thank you."

(10)

Agent: Dobrze, **proszę o chwilę cierpliwości** [Request: Time Management] "Agent: Well, **please be patient for a moment**"

Klient: **Dobrze.** [acceptRequest, wymiar: Time Management] "Client: **Okay.**"

(11)

Agent: (...)**proponuję, abyśmy tutaj (...) wspólnie, w trakcie trwania połączenia, wystawili, wystawiły reklamację do tej faktury, dobrze?** [Offer: Task] "Agent: (...) **I propose that we here (...) together, during the call, issue a claim to this invoice, alright?**"

Klient: **Dobrze.** [acceptOffer: Task] "Client: **Alright.**"

(12)

Agent: Czterdzieści trzy. Tak? "Agent: Forty-three. Yes?"

Klient: Tak. "Client: Yes."

Agent: **Dobrze.** [contactIndication: Contact Management] "Agent: **Go on.**"

6.3 "Tak"

The third word we wish to consider is the word "tak" in Polish, which may be roughly translated as "yes" in English.

In Polish "tak" can be used in a variety of situations, including to answer yes or to acknowledge understanding. It can also be used as a discourse marker to indicate agreement, to signal a willingness to continue the conversation, or to show politeness. In English, "yes" is generally used to answer a question or to indicate agreement or affirmation.

The use of "tak" in Polish can also depend on the social and cultural context of the conversation. For example, "tak" can be used to indicate politeness or deference to a speaker who is perceived to be of a higher social status. In English, "yes" is generally used regardless of social context, but can be used to express politeness or informality depending on the situation. The word "tak" in Polish can also imply a level of certainty or emphasis in agreement or affirmation. It can also suggest that the speaker is more committed to their agreement or affirmation than "yes" in English. In contrast, "yes" in English is generally more neutral in terms of emphasis or certainty. We have distinguished four different dialogue functions (Confirm - 739 cases, Contact Indication - 1311, Auto/Allo Positive - 257, Agreement - 326) for "tak" illustrated in (13)-(16) below.

(13)

Klient: **Autobus 121 odjeżdża z rogu Podleśnej w kierunku Wrzeciona, prawda?** [checkQuestion: Task] "Client: **Bus 121 leaves from the corner of Podleśna towards Wrzecion, correct?**"

Agent: **Tak.** [Confirm: Task] "Agent: **Yes.**"

(14)

Klient: A czy... "Client: And is..."

Agent: **Tak?** [contactIndication: Contact Management] Agent: **Yes?**

Klient: Czy to wtedy (yy) przyjdzie ktoś osobiście... "Client: Is it then (yy) that someone is going to come in person...

(15)

Agent: Wystawiła pani trójkąt i co najmniej sto metrów przed pojazdem pani postawiła. "Agent: You pulled out a warning triangle and put it out at least a hundred metres in front of your vehicle."

Klient: **Tak.** [alloPositive: Allo-Feedback] "Client: **Yes.**"

(16)

Klient: (yy) Aż tyle mam możliwości. "Client: (yy) So many possibilities."

Agent: **Tak.** [Agreement: Task] "Agent: [Yes.]

7 Conclusion / General discussion

Dialogue act annotation involves assigning a specific communicative function or speech act to each utterance in a conversation. The process of annotating dialogue acts can be affected by differences in language between Polish and English. In Polish honorifics and inflection are commonly used to convey meaning, which can make it difficult to accurately identify and annotate dialogue acts. The complexity of Polish sentence structures can also present a challenge. Morphologically rich languages, like Polish, have more inflections and grammatical markers that can complicate the annotation process. Additionally, polysemous words can create confusion and ambiguity when trying to distinguish between multiple meanings. To address these challenges, clear guidelines and instructions should be provided to annotators, and multiple rounds of reviews and revisions should be performed to ensure accuracy and consistency. Context and cultural norms can also be helpful in disambiguating the meaning of polysemous words.

The ISO standard serves as a suitable framework for annotating dialogues in different languages. The existing categories provided a means to address cases where language differences emerged, while considering the contextual factors played a crucial role in reaching final decisions. To ensure the adoption of specific solutions, it is important to maintain a consistent approach to dimension recognition. Given the variations across languages, the ISO standard should have a well-defined theoretical foundation, as English examples may not always be sufficient.

To enable effective utilization of the model, guidelines are necessary, empowering annotators to conduct a comprehensive analysis that incorporates both conceptual frameworks and specific textual structures. This entails providing clear and practical definitions of annotated categories, establishing a solid theoretical basis, as well as discussing illustrative examples.

References

Ju D Apresjan. 1974. *Leksičeskaja semantika: Sinonimičeskije sredstva jazyka*. Nauka.

Andrzej Bogusławski. 1976. O zasadach rejestracji jednostek języka. *Poradnik językowy*, 8(342):356–364.

Harry Bunt, Jan Alexandersson, Jean Carletta, Jae-Woong Choe, Alex Chengyu Fang, Koiti Hasida, Kiyong Lee, Volha Petukhova, Andrei Popescu-Belis, Laurent Romary, Claudia Soria, and David Traum. 2010a. Towards an ISO Standard for Dialogue Act Annotation. In *Seventh conference on International Language Resources and Evaluation (LREC'10)*, La Valette, Malta.

Harry Bunt, Jan Alexandersson, Jean Carletta, Jae-Woong Choe, Alex Chengyu Fang, Koiti Hasida, Kiyong Lee, Volha Petukhova, Andrei Popescu-Belis, Laurent Romary, Claudia Soria, and David Traum. 2010b. Towards an ISO standard for dialogue act annotation. In *Proceedings of the Seventh International Conference on Language Resources and Evaluation (LREC'10)*, Valletta, Malta. European Language Resources Association (ELRA).

Harry Bunt, Jan Alexandersson, Jae-Woong Choe, Alex Chengyu Fang, Koiti Hasida, Volha Petukhova, Andrei Popescu-Belis, and David Traum. 2012. ISO 24617-2: A semantically-based standard for dialogue annotation. In *Proceedings of the Eighth International Conference on Language Resources and Evaluation (LREC'12)*, pages 430–437, Istanbul, Turkey. European Language Resources Association (ELRA).

Harry Bunt, Volha Petukhova, Emer Gilmartin, Catherine Pelachaud, Alex Chengyu Fang, Simon Keizer, and Laurent Prévot. 2020. The iso standard for dialogue act annotation, second edition. In *International Conference on Language Resources and Evaluation*.

Harry Bunt, Volha Petukhova, Andrei Malchanau, Kars Wijnhoven, and Alex Fang. 2016. The DialogBank. In *Proceedings of the Tenth International Conference on Language Resources and Evaluation (LREC'16)*, pages 3151–3158, Portorož, Slovenia. European Language Resources Association (ELRA).

Harry Bunt, James Pustejovsky, and Kiyong Lee. 2018. Towards an ISO standard for the annotation of quantification. In *Proceedings of the Eleventh International Conference on Language Resources and Evaluation (LREC 2018)*, Miyazaki, Japan. European Language Resources Association (ELRA).

Shammur Absar Chowdhury, Evgeny Stepanov, and Giuseppe Riccardi. 2016. Transfer of corpus-specific dialogue act annotation to ISO standard: Is it worth it? In *Proceedings of the Tenth International Conference on Language Resources and Evaluation (LREC'16)*, pages 132–135, Portorož, Slovenia. European Language Resources Association (ELRA).

Chengyu Fang, Jing Cao, Harry Bunt, and Xiaoyue Liu. 2012. The annotation of the switchboard corpus with the new iso standard for dialogue act analysis. In *Proceedings of the Eighth Joint ACL-ISO Workshop on Interoperable Semantic Annotation*. Eighth Joint ACL-ISO Workshop on Interoperable Semantic Annotation ; Conference date: 03-10-2012 Through 05-10-2012.

Emer Gilmartin, Christian Saam, Brendan Spillane, Maria O'Reilly, Ketong Su, Arturo Calvo, Loredana Cerrato, Killian Levacher, Nick Campbell, and Vincent Wade. 2018. The ADELE corpus of dyadic social text conversations:dialog act annotation with ISO 24617-2. In *Proceedings of the Eleventh International Conference on Language Resources and Evaluation (LREC 2018)*, Miyazaki, Japan. European Language Resources Association (ELRA).

Ewa Gruszczyńska, Małgorzata Guławska-Gawkowska, and Anna Szczęsny. 2019. *Translatoryczne i dyskursywne oblicza komunikacji*. Instytutu Lingwistyki Stosowanej WLS UW.

Simon Keizer, Harry Bunt, and Volha Petukhova. 2011. *Multidimensional Dialogue Management*, pages 57–86. Springer Berlin Heidelberg, Berlin, Heidelberg.

George Lakoff. 2008. *Women, fire, and dangerous things: What categories reveal about the mind*. University of Chicago press.

Barbara Lewandowska-Tomaszczyk and Marcel Thelen. 2013. Translation and meaning part 10.

Essa T. Mohammed. 2009. Polysemy as a lexical problem in translation.

Thi-Lan Ngo, Son-Bao Pham, Khac-Linh Pham, Xuan-Hieu Phan, and Minh-Son Cao. 2017. Dialogue act segmentation for vietnamese human-human conversational texts. In *2017 9th International Conference on Knowledge and Systems Engineering (KSE)*, pages 203–208.

Marcin Oleksy, Jan Wieczorek, Dorota Drużyłowska, Julia Klyus, Aleksandra Domogała, Krzysztof Hwaszcz, Hanna Kędzierska, Daria Mikoś, and Anita Wróż. 2022. Diabiz.kom - towards a polish dialogue act corpus based on iso 24617-2 standard. In *International Conference on Computational Linguistics*.

Mateusz Arkadiusz Ostalak. 2019. *A comparative analysis of grammatical structures and vocabulary in Polish and English Facebook chats*. Katowice.

Volha Petukhova, Harry Bunt, Andrei Malchanau, and Ramkumar Aruchamy. 2015. Experimenting with grounding strategies in dialogue. *SEMDIAL 2015 goDIAL*, page 198.

Volha Petukhova, Martin Gropp, Dietrich Klakow, Gregor Eigner, Mario Topf, Stefan Srb, Petr Motlicek, Blaise Potard, John Dines, Olivier Deroo, Ronny Egeler, Uwe Meinz, Steffen Liersch, and Anna

Schmidt. 2014. The DBOX corpus collection of spoken human-human and human-machine dialogues. In *Proceedings of the Ninth International Conference on Language Resources and Evaluation (LREC'14)*, pages 252–258, Reykjavik, Iceland. European Language Resources Association (ELRA).

Piotr Pęzik, Gosia Krawentek, Sylwia Karasińska, Paweł Wilk, Paulina Rybińska, Anna Cichosz, Angelika Peljak-Lapinska, Mikołaj Deckert, and Michał Adamczyk. 2022. Diabiz – an annotated corpus of polish call center dialogs. In *International Conference on Language Resources and Evaluation*.

Goran Schmidt. 2008. Polysemy in translation - selecting the right sense.

Purificação Silvano, Mariana Damova, Giedrė Valūnaitė Olekeviienė, Chaya Liebeskind, C. Chiarcos, Dimitar Trajanov, Ciprian-Octavian Truică, Elena Simona Apostol, and Anna Bączkowska. 2022. Iso-based annotated multilingual parallel corpus for discourse markers. In *International Conference on Language Resources and Evaluation*.

Towards Referential Transparent Annotations of Quantified Noun Phrases

Andy Lücking
Université Paris Cité
Case 7031 - 5, rue Thomas Mann, 75205 Paris cedex 13, France
Goethe University Frankfurt
Robert-Mayer-Straße 10, 60325 Frankfurt am Main, Germany
lueecking@em.uni-frankfurt.de

Abstract

Using recent developments in count noun quantification, namely *Referential Transparency Theory* (RTT), the basic structure for annotating quantification in the nominal domain according to RTT is presented. The paper discusses core ideas of RTT, derives the abstract annotation syntax, and exemplifies annotations of quantified noun phrases partly in comparison to QuantML.

1 Introduction

The collection of interoperable semantic annotation standards known as the *Semantic Annotation Framework* (SemAF) includes an annotation schema for the annotation of quantification phenomena called QuantML (Bunt, 2019b; Bunt et al., 2022). QuantML draws on work in formal and computational semantics, in particular Generalized Quantifier Theory (Barwise and Cooper, 1981), Discourse Representation Theory (Kamp and Reyle, 1993), and neo-Davidsonian event semantics (Davidson, 1967; Parsons, 1990). It aims at a considerable if not complete coverage of natural language quantification.

With respect to quantified noun phrases (QNPs) – that is, noun phrases which involve a quantifier word – an alternative to Generalized Quantifier Theory (GQT) has recently been developed in terms of *Referential Transparency Theory* (RTT; Lücking and Ginzburg, 2022).[1] RTT draws its main motivation from data of natural language use as observed in dialogical interactions, where higher-order denotations postulated by GQT do not seem to be confirmed. Hence, RTT pursues a witness-based approach to quantification, which arguably simplifies the representation of quantification phenomena. QuantRTT aims at an annotation schema which makes the RTT approach available for annotation.

The paper is organized as follows. Section 2 introduces the key ideas of RTT that are needed to understand the annotation approach outlined in section 3. The interpretation of QuantRTT annotations in the RTT framework is briefly covered in section 4. Some phenomena outside the current scope of QuantRTT are discussed in section 5. We conclude in section 6.

2 Brief Primer into RTT

Perhaps the most consequential feature of RTT is that quantification with quantificational determiners and nouns happens entirely within the noun phrase. In other words, a QNP such as *many goldfish* is interpreted without reference to a so-called scope set (the property donated by the verb phrase in GQT). RTT makes crucial use of the fact that QNP contents seem to be readily structured entities, as is revealed by their anaphoric potential. Consider (1): The initial sentence introduces a QNP (*few environmentalists*). The few environmentalists that actually came to the rally – the *reference set* (refset) – are picked up by the plural pronoun in (1a). However, two additional sets become accessible: the "refset environmentalists" seem to be drawn from a larger group of environmentalists – the *maximal set* (max set) –, which is picked out by the plural pronoun phrase in (1b). The plural pronoun in (1c), finally, picks out those environmentalists that did *not* came to the rally: the *complement set* (compset).[2]

(1) Only few environmentalists came to the rally.

a. But they raised their placards defiantly.

[1] "Transparency" here – a feature of the representation of noun phrase contents – is not to be confused with transparency of QuantML, where it refers to the instantiation of a meta-model (Bunt et al., 2022, §4.3).

[2] The examples in (1) are constructed for the sake of brevity but follow the pattern of corpus examples of maxset/refset/compset anaphora; see, e.g., Del Negro (2020).

Proceedings of the 19th Joint ACL - ISO Workshop on Interoperable Semantic Annotation, pages 47–55
June 20, 2023. ©2023 Association for Computational Linguistics

b. Although they all received an invitation.

c. They went to a football game instead.

Note that compset anaphora is only licensed under certain conditions (see, e.g., Nouwen, 2003). RTT offers a *horror vacui*-based explanation here, drawing on empty refsets (Lücking and Ginzburg, 2022, §4.3) – see (4) below.

Assuming that the "QNP anatomy" (a phrase we owe to Cooper, 2013) indeed hosts a set triplet, RTT develops the following QNP structure:

(2)
$$\begin{bmatrix} \text{q-params} : \begin{bmatrix} \text{refset} & : \textit{Set(Ind)} \\ \text{compset} & : \textit{Set(Ind)} \\ \text{maxset} & : \textit{Set(Ind)} \\ \text{c1} & : \overrightarrow{\textit{PType}}(\text{maxset}) \\ \text{c2} & : \text{union(maxset,refset,compset)} \end{bmatrix} \\ \text{q-cond} \quad : \textit{Rel}(|\text{q-params.refset}|, |\text{q-params.compset}|) \\ \text{q-persp} \quad : \text{refset} = \emptyset \vee \text{refset} \neq \emptyset \vee \text{ none} \end{bmatrix}$$

RTT is formulated within a type theory with records (Cooper and Ginzburg, 2015; Cooper, 2023). The arrow indicates a plural predicate type (*PType*), that is, a predicate that expects a set-valued argument. Condition c2 simply states that refset and compset add up to the maxset. Obviously, the structure in (2) provides suitable antecedents for the above-given range of anaphora. The value of condition c1 is donated by the predicate type of the head noun (e.g., *environmentalist*, *goldfish*), which is distributed over all maxset members (and thereby over refset and compset). The quantificational workhorse is the quantifier condition "q-cond": it captures what can be called the descriptive meaning of a QNP. For instance, the q-cond of *many* states that the refset is larger than the compset (|refset| > |compset|). The quantificational condition of *all* has it that the compset is empty, or equivalently, that refset and maxset coincide. Hence, q-cond not only expresses NP-internal quantification (i.e., quantification without a scope set from the VP), it also implements quantifiers as "sieves", a metaphor due to Barwise and Cooper (1981). This is achieved since RTT is denotationally underpinned by sets of ordered set bipartitions, mathematical structures which correspond to inversely coupled pairs of the elements of the power set of the head noun's denotation.

(3) **Ordered set bipartition.** An ordered set bipartition b of a set s is a pair of disjoint subsets of s including the empty set such that the union of these subsets is s. We refer to the set of all possible ordered set bipartitions of a set s as the *set of ordered set bipartitions.*

For example, let the denotation [↓] of the type *Bicycle* be a set of three bicycles: [↓ Bicycle] = {🚲, 🚲, 🚲}. Then function p returns the set of ordered set bipartitions:

(4) p([↓ Bicycle]) = {⟨∅, {🚲, 🚲, 🚲}⟩,
⟨{🚲}, {🚲, 🚲}⟩,
⟨{🚲}, {🚲, 🚲}⟩,
⟨{🚲}, {🚲, 🚲}⟩,
⟨{🚲, 🚲}, {🚲}⟩,
⟨{🚲, 🚲}, {🚲}⟩,
⟨{🚲, 🚲}, {🚲}⟩,
⟨{🚲, 🚲, 🚲}, ∅⟩}

Each ordered set bipartition in the set of ordered bipartitions is structured in the form ⟨refset, compset⟩. Accordingly, the last ordered set bipartition in (4), the one with an empty compset, is the denotation of *every bicycle* in the sample universe. The first bipartition, the one with an empty refset, corresponds to *no*-type NPs. Those bipartitions which have more elements in the refset than in the compset are the denotations of *many*-type NPs. Note that the (hypothesized) semantic universal of *conservativity* (Keenan and Stavi, 1986) ("lives on" in the terminology of Barwise and Cooper 1981) is an immediate consequence.

Feature q-persp in (2) indicates whether the bipartition with the empty refset is part of a QNP's denotation; if so, its feature value is "refset = ∅"; otherwise "refset ≠ ∅". NPs for which q-persp is not applicable – such as proper names – have no q-persp value ("none"). Thus, the q-persp value is denotationally well-founded and regiments compset anaphora: the compset is available as antecedent only if "q-persp : refset = ∅".

Any NP-internal approach to quantification needs to say something about how a QNP combines with a verb phrase (VP) into a sentence. RTT – in contrast to GQT – adopts the standard (and intuitively pleasing) notion of predication: the verb predicates of its arguments. To be more precise: VP content applies to the refsets of its arguments. That is, the meaning of a sentence like *Every dog barks* is compositionally derived as illustrated in (5), abbreviated to the necessary degree (the pair of a situation and a situation type is an *Austinian proposition* (Ginzburg, 2012); label "q-params" is abbreviated "q-p" in some paths here and in the following for reasons of space):

(5)
$$\begin{bmatrix} \text{q-params} : \begin{bmatrix} \text{refset} : \textit{Set(Ind)} \\ \text{c1} \quad : \overrightarrow{\textit{dog}}(\text{refset}) \end{bmatrix} \\ \text{cont} = \begin{bmatrix} \text{sit=s0} : \textit{Rec} \\ \text{sit-type=} \begin{bmatrix} \text{q-cond} : \text{compset=} \ \emptyset \\ \text{nucl} : \overrightarrow{\textit{bark}}(\text{q-p.refset}) \\ \text{anti-nucl} : \neg\overrightarrow{\textit{bark}}(\text{q-p.compset}) \end{bmatrix} \end{bmatrix} \end{bmatrix}$$

Note that (5) involves "anti-predication" of the compset. Postulating multi-dimensional denotations is not uncommon in semantics, Rooth (2016), for instance, argues for a related move.

Since a plural type takes a set of individuals as argument, the question arises on how exactly the predicate relates to the members of the set. The predicate *bark* in (5) obviously distributes to every single dog from the refset. This is distinct from collective predicates like *gather*, which apply to sets of individuals, and predicates like *carry-a-piano*, which, when asserted of a set of people, can be understood in a distributive or a collective way, and anything in between (Scha, 1984). Spelling out the details of distributivity is a bit involved (see Lücking, 2022, Sec. 2.5), therefore QuantRTT offers simple notational abbreviations, following the subtyping relation in (6):

(6)

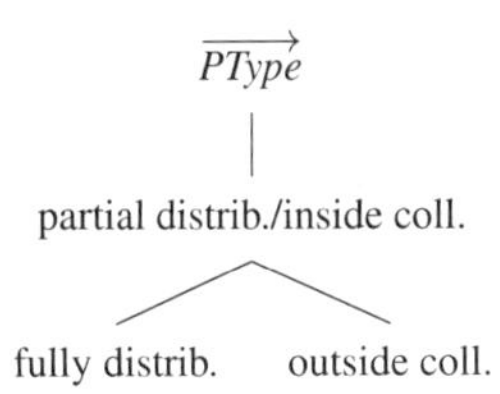

The general plural type imposes no restriction onto its interpretation, whereas fully distributive and outside collective ones require what their names suggest. The types in the middle express that a plural predicate applies to individuals and to any subgroups of the refset (this is RTT's counterpart to *covers*, lattices of subsets under set inclusion). Since these substructures can be seen from the perspective of either distributivity (in terms of partiality) or collectivity (in terms of inside collections), there are two possible ways to name these subtypes.

Let us briefly illustrate matters by means of a simple example: *Every dog chased a cat.* This sentence can be used to describe situations of different kinds, namely a situation where (i) a bunch of dogs together chased a cat (outside collective), (ii) each dog from the bunch chased a different cat (fully distributive), or (iii) some dogs chased in teams (i.e., there is more than one cat but the number of cats is less than the number of dogs).

How does this exposition fit to so-called narrow and wide scope readings ($\forall\exists$ vs. $\exists\forall$)? It does not, since scope is replaced by *dependent* interpretations of QNPs (Zeevat, 2018; Ginzburg, 2012), which apply *in situ* and introduce a function. The relevant content parts for the *every-dog-chased-a-cat* example are shown in (7). The subject QNP introduces a refset (and a suitable q-cond), as usual. The object QNP introduces a function f which associates an individual x with a cat z. The nucleus distributively applies the predicate and the function to the subject's refset, which provides entities x (dogs in our example) as input for f, which in turn returns a cat each (i.e., an individual of type *cat*).[3]

(7)
$$\begin{bmatrix} \text{q-params} : \begin{bmatrix} \text{refset} : \textit{Set(Ind)} \\ \text{c1} : \overset{\text{dist}}{\overrightarrow{\text{dog}}}(\text{refset}) \\ \text{f} : ([\text{x} : \textit{Ind}]) \begin{bmatrix} \text{z=f(x)} : \textit{Ind} \\ \text{c0} : \text{cat(z)} \end{bmatrix} \end{bmatrix} \\ \text{nucl} : \overset{\text{dist}}{\overrightarrow{\text{chase}}}(\text{q-p.refset,f(q-p.refset)}) \\ \text{anti-nucl} : \neg\overset{\text{dist}}{\overrightarrow{\text{chase}}}(\text{q-p.compset,f(q-p.compset)}) \end{bmatrix}$$

The representational format of RTT – albeit presumably uncommon to most readers – is arguably more transparent than equivalent formulæ of second order predicate logic. Moreover, there is a systematic distinction between *quantification* (q-params) and *predication* (nucl). For this reason, the domain of markables of QuantRTT is more restricted than that of QuantML.

This leaves a final and potentially intricate issue: definiteness. Coming from a dialogical point of view, RTT employs a "referential bookkeeping mechanism", following HPSG-related work (Ginzburg and Purver, 2012). The crucial idea is that certain nominal expressions are expected to be *witnessed* while others are "quantified away". This is expressed in terms of two sets of parameters, *dgb-params* and *q-params*. Elements within the dialogue gameboard parameters (dgb-params; a generalization of Kaplanian indices) are expected

[3]Imposing further constraints on f bring about, for instance, interpretations for *same* (f constant) and *different* (f injective) (Lücking, 2022, p. 78).

to be instantiated by an object or a set of objects known to the speaker(s), whereas quantificational parameters (q-params) need not have a specific witness. Note that during dialogical clarification interaction the status of belonging to either dgb-params or q-params can switch.

3 Annotating with QuantRTT

We follow the general approach of QuantML and conceive a markable m and an annotation s as an entity structure $\langle m, s\rangle$. Markables are the strings making up noun phrases. Annotations are derived from the above-introduced QNP anatomy. The relation between two or more entity structures is captured in terms of a link structure. The inventory of QuantRTT looks as follows:

1. *Entities* have the following features, where the corresponding feature values are given after the colon:
   - `q-cond`: `compset=empty` (for *every*, *all*), `refset=empty` (for *no*), potentially negated by "!" [see (13b) below], a condition of the form '`refset` R `compset`', with $R \in \{\leq, <, \ll, =, \geq, >, \gg\}$, or `card=`$n$ ($n \in \mathbb{R}$)[4]
   - `status`: `dgb`, `q` (assigning no value corresponds to "unknown")
   - `ptype`: the predicate of the head noun in question
   - `distrib`: `full`, `part`, `coll` (assigning no value corresponds to "unknown" and allows for any interpretation according to (6))
2. *Links* connect dependent NPs with the NP they depend on *via* the value of the eponymous feature `dep(endent)_on`.

Note that we omit the annotation of q-persp since it is not involved in quantification proper but mainly regiments compset anaphora.

Comparing the inventories of QuantML and QuantRTT, we are aware of the following correspondences ($\sim$):

- `ptype` $\sim$ `pred`
- `maxset` $\sim$ reference domain or context set (Westerståhl, 1985) (the source domain corresponds to a type's denotation "$[\downarrow]$" and is not part of the annotation)
- `status` $\sim$ `determinacy`
- `distrib=full` $\sim$ `distr=individual`, `distrib=coll` $\sim$ `collective`

The attributes `q-cond` and `involvement` have some functional commonalities, but do not completely correspond to each other, as can be seen, for instance, with NP negation – see (11) and (13b) below. Phenomena such as inverse linking, cover interpretations or group quantification are captured in terms of dependencies (`dep_on`) in combination with `distrib` (cf. Section 2).

All QuantRTT features have direct counterparts in the QNP anatomy. The remainder of this section presents a few examples in order to showcase QuantRTT in action.

A famous example for scope readings is given in (8), discussed by Bunt (2020, p. 4):

(8) Everybody in this room speaks two languages.

The reading where *two languages* is interpreted in the scope of *everybody* (i.e., the reading where there might be different pairs languages for different persons) is annotated in QuantML as follows:

```
<entity xml:id="x1" target="#m1"
↪ involvement="all" definiteness="det"
↪ pred="person"/>
<entity xml:id="x2" target="#m3"
↪ involvement="2" definiteness="indet"
↪ pred="language">
<scoping arg1="#x1" arg2="#x2"
↪ scopeRel="wider"/>
```

The same reading is obtained in QuantRTT by annotating the markable *two languages* as a functional NP which depends on *everybody in this room*:

```
<entity xml:id="x1" target="#m1"
↪ q-cond="compset=empty" status="dgb"
↪ ptype="person"/>
<entity xml:id="x2" target="#m3"
↪ q-cond="card=2" status="q"
↪ ptype="language" dep_on="#x1"
↪ distrib="full">
```

[4]We restrict cardinalities to rational numbers in order to account for examples such *Kim ate* $1\frac{1}{3}$ *pizzas*, pointed out by an anonymous reviewer. Of course, this restriction can be extended to real numbers, if needed.

The value `distrib="full"` indicates that the dependency holds for every single element of the governing NP's denotation. This annotation represents the RTT structures in figures 1 (for *everybody*) and 2 (for *two languages*). The sentential meaning is obtained by relating both structures with the *speaking* relation in such a way that the functional NP is distributionally applied to the refset of the universally quantified NP and is shown in Figure 3. Note, however, that such sentential structures are not part of the scope of markables of QuantRTT, which is confined to the QNP representations in figures 1 and 2, complying to RTT's separation of quantification and verbal predication. The proposition in figure 3 is nonetheless compositionally derived in grammar – HPSG$_{\text{TTR}}$ (Cooper, 2008; Ginzburg, 2012; Lücking et al., 2021) – by using standard constructions such as determiner–noun rules and head–subject rules, and lexical entries for quantifiers like that for *every* in (9) which passes a distributivity marker via its (count) head noun (Beghelli and Stowell, 1997) to the predicating VP, enforcing a (partially) distributive interpretation.

(9)

$$\left[\begin{array}{l}\text{phon} : /\text{every}/ \\ \text{cat} : \left[\begin{array}{l}\text{head} : \left[\begin{array}{ll}\text{pos=det} & : \mathit{PoS} \\ \text{agr} & : \left[\text{num=sg} : \mathit{Num}\right] \\ \text{count=+} & : \mathit{Binary}\end{array}\right] \\ \text{spec} : \left\langle \left[\text{cat} : \left[\text{head} : \left[\begin{array}{ll}\text{pos=n} & : \mathit{PoS} \\ \text{distr=+} & : \mathit{Binary}\end{array}\right]\right]\right]\right\rangle\end{array}\right] \\ \text{q-params} : \left[\begin{array}{l}\text{maxset} : \mathit{Set(Ind)} \\ \text{refset} : \mathit{Set(Ind)} \\ \text{compset} : \mathit{Set(Ind)} \\ \text{c1} : \text{union(refset,compset,maxset)} \\ \text{q-cond} : |\text{refset}| = |\text{maxset}|\end{array}\right]\end{array}\right]$$

Dependent interpretations also apply to inverse linking arising from prepositional modification as in (10) (Bunt, 2020, p. 7):

(10) Two students from every university [...]

```
<entity xml:id="x1" target="#m1"
↪ q-cond="card=2" dep_on="#x2"
↪ distrib="full" ptype="student">
<entity xml:id="x2" target="m3"
↪ q-cond="compset=empty"
↪ ptype="university">
```

Since the sentence does not carry enough information about the status of the discourse referents (`dgb` vs. `q`), it is left unspecified.

RTT also offers a compositional treatment of *Not*-type QNPs, such as in (11) (taken from Bunt 2020, p. 7):

(11) Not all the unions accept the proposal.

The basic idea is that *not*, when used as noun phrase negation, inverts the q-cond and q-persp relations of the noun phrase (Lücking and Ginzburg, 2019). (12b) exemplifies the relation of the negated NP from (11) to the positive one in (12a).

(12) a.

$$\left[\begin{array}{ll}\text{refset} & : \mathit{Set(Ind)} \\ \text{compset} & : \mathit{Set(Ind)} \\ \text{maxset} & : \mathit{Set(Ind)} \\ \text{c1} & : \text{union(refset,compset,maxset)} \\ \text{c2} & : \overrightarrow{\text{unions}}\text{(maxset)} \\ \text{q-cond} & : \text{compset} = \emptyset \\ \text{q-persp} & : \text{refset} \neq \emptyset\end{array}\right]$$

b.

$$\left[\begin{array}{ll}\text{refset} & : \mathit{Set(Ind)} \\ \text{compset} & : \mathit{Set(Ind)} \\ \text{maxset} & : \mathit{Set(Ind)} \\ \text{c1} & : \text{union(refset,compset,maxset)} \\ \text{c2} & : \overrightarrow{\text{unions}}\text{(maxset)} \\ \text{q-cond} & : \text{compset} \neq \emptyset \\ \text{q-persp} & : \text{refset} = \emptyset\end{array}\right]$$

Note that(12b) correctly accounts for the interaction of *not* and compset anaphora in a compositional manner.

The annotation of (12b) is straightforward (ignoring q-persp, however), using "!" to denote the *not*-operator (thus != is the same as $\neq$):

(13) a. "all the unions":

```
<entity q-cond="compset=empty">
```

b. "not all the unions":

```
<entity q-cond="compset!=empty">
```

Likewise for other relationships (e.g., $\leq$ of *fewer than* maps to $>$ of *not fewer than*, and so forth).

4 Interpreting Annotations

Since annotations are derived from a QNP anatomy, annotations can be mapped onto either the basic QNP structure in (2) or the functional one in (7) of RTT, as illustrated in figures 1 and 2. Note that in line with RTT's NP-internal approach to nominal quantification and the distinction between quantification and verbal predication, annotations in QuantRTT do not involve verb phrases (i.e., figure 3).

$$
\begin{bmatrix}
\text{dgb-params} : \begin{bmatrix}
\text{maxset} & : \mathit{Set(Ind)} \\
\text{refset} & : \mathit{Set(Ind)} \\
\text{compset} & : \mathit{Set(Ind)} \\
\text{c2} & : \text{union(refset,compset,maxset)} \\
\text{c1} & : \overset{\text{dist}}{\overrightarrow{\text{person}}}\text{(maxset)} \\
\text{qcond} & : |\text{dgb-params.refset}| = |\text{dgb-params.maxset}|
\end{bmatrix}
\end{bmatrix}
$$

Figure 1: Representation of *Everybody*'s dgb-params.

$$
\begin{bmatrix}
\text{q-params} : \begin{bmatrix}
\text{f} : ([\text{x} : \mathit{Ind}]) \begin{bmatrix}
\text{refset=f(x)} & : \mathit{Set(Ind)} \\
\text{maxset} & : \mathit{Set(Ind)} \\
\text{compset} & : \mathit{Set(Ind)} \\
\text{c2} & : \text{union(refset,compset,maxset)} \\
\text{c1} & : \overset{\text{dist}}{\overrightarrow{\text{language}}}\text{(maxset)} \\
\text{q-cond} & : |\text{refset}| = 2
\end{bmatrix}
\end{bmatrix}
\end{bmatrix}
$$

Figure 2: Dependent interpretation of *two languages*'s q-params.

$$
\begin{bmatrix}
\text{dgb-params} : & \begin{bmatrix}
\text{refset-sbj} & : \mathit{Set(Ind)} \\
\text{compset-sbj} & : \mathit{Set(Ind)} \\
\text{maxset-sbj} & : \mathit{Set(Ind)} \\
\text{c0} & : \text{union(refset-sbj,compset-sbj,maxset-sbj)} \\
\text{c1} & : \overrightarrow{\text{person}}\text{(maxset-sbj)} \\
\text{q-cond-sbj} & : |\text{refset-sbj}| = |\text{maxset-sbj}|
\end{bmatrix} \\
\text{cont} \quad = & \begin{bmatrix}
\text{sit} = \text{s1} : \mathit{Rec} \\
\text{sit-type} = \begin{bmatrix}
\text{q-params} : \begin{bmatrix}
\text{f} : ([\text{x} : \mathit{Ind}]) \begin{bmatrix}
\text{refset-obj=f(x)} : \mathit{Set(Ind)} \\
\text{maxset-obj} : \mathit{Set(Ind)} \\
\text{compset-obj} : \mathit{Set(Ind)} \\
\text{c2} : \text{union(refset-obj,compset-obj,maxset-obj)} \\
\text{c1} : \overset{\text{dist}}{\overrightarrow{\text{language}}}\text{(maxset-obj)} \\
\text{q-cond-obj} : |\text{refset-obj}| = 2
\end{bmatrix}
\end{bmatrix} \\
\text{nucl} \quad : \overset{\text{dist}}{\overrightarrow{\text{speak}}}\text{(refset-sbj, f(refset-sbj))} \\
\text{anti-nucl} : \neg\overset{\text{dist}}{\overrightarrow{\text{speak}}}\text{(compset-sbj, f(compset-sbj))}
\end{bmatrix} : \mathit{RecType}
\end{bmatrix} : \mathit{Prop}
\end{bmatrix}
$$

Figure 3: Sentence meaning of *Everybody speaks two languages.*

5 Discussion

An anonymous reviewer brought up the following participation example:

(14) Three of the twenty-two students failed the exam.

From the perspective of RTT, (14) involves two cardinality restrictions, one on the refset (viz., "card=3") and one on the maxset ("card=22"). The latter, however, can not yet be expressed in QuantRTT, simply because the annotation inventory (see section 3) lacks a corresponding annotation label. This can easily be fixed in future versions, but will still not capture recursive participant structures as in (15):

(15) Three of the twenty-two students among the forty-eight participants failed the exam.

We are not aware of how (or whether) such examples are to be annotated in QuantML, but we imagine a nested annotation drawing on `involvement` and `sourceDomain`.

The empirical phenomena that underlie the development of RTT involve count nouns. Hence, currently RTT has not much to say about mass nouns and quantification with substances yet, as involved in (16) (Bunt, 2020, p. 6).

(16) The boys drank all the milk in the fridge.

However, given that RTT is formulated in a type theory with records, it seems to be straightforward to follow psychological work (e.g., Rips and Hespos, 2015) and introduce a type *Subst(ance)* alongside *Ind(ividual)*. Given this, it seems that RTT's basic mechanisms can be adapted to substances, in which case the q-cond acts like a sieve on what can be called "refmass" and "compmass":

(17) a. The boys drank most of the milk in the fridge.

b. The boys drank as much of the milk in the fridge as they did not.

On this view, classifiers like *three cups* (*of milk*) induce a type shift from *Subst* to *Ind*.

Furthermore, natural languages provide resources like the English adverbial modifier *twice* to quantify over events (Bunt, 2019b, p. 8):

(18) Two of the children called twice.

Intuitively, (18) says that there have been two calling events by two children (from a certain maxset). RTT has not dealt with temporal or spatial quantification yet. However, a potential direction to account for (18) shall be indicated, drawing on the notion of *string type* (Fernando 2007; Cooper 2023, §2.2). A string type is a concatenation of types. It can be thought of as a flip book and is used for temporally structuring an event into sub-events. Accordingly, potential witnesses of string types are series of situations. Event quantification on this view can be seen as a mechanism of constructing a string of copies (of a number determined by the descriptive meaning of the temporal modifier in question) from a given situation type. Notating the string type '$\overrightarrow{\text{call}}(X)^\frown\overrightarrow{\text{call}}(X)$' simply by a superscript indicating the number of copies (i.e., by '$\overrightarrow{\text{call}}(X)^2$'), (18) is analyzed as follows (omitting details not relevant to the issue at stake):

(19)
$$\left[\begin{array}{ll} \text{q-params} : & \left[\begin{array}{l}\text{refset} : \mathit{Set(Ind)} \\ \text{c0} : \overrightarrow{\text{child}}(\text{refset})\end{array}\right] \\ \text{cont} = & \left[\begin{array}{ll}\text{sit} = s_1 s_2 & \\ \text{sit-type} = & \left[\begin{array}{l}\text{q-cond} : |\text{q-params.refset}| = 2 \\ \text{nucl} : \overrightarrow{\text{call}}(\text{q-params.refset})^2\end{array}\right]\end{array}\right]\end{array}\right]$$

Note that *sit* now consists of a series of two events, s_1 and s_2.

It is finally noteworthy – since it has been raised as an issue by Bunt (2019b, §7) – that a type theory provides a straightforward analysis of propositional attitude verbs like *believe* or *seek*. Since propositions *are* types (Martin-Löf, 1984), intensional verbs denote a relation between individuals and types, as shown in (20), following Cooper (2005, p. 341).

(20) a. Vic seeks a unicorn.

b.
$$\left[\begin{array}{ll} \text{x} & : \mathit{Ind} \\ \text{c0} & : \text{named(x, "Vic")} \\ \text{p} = \left[\begin{array}{l}\text{y} : \mathit{Ind} \\ \text{c1} : \text{unicorn(y)}\end{array}\right] & : \mathit{RecType} \\ \text{c2} & : \text{seek(x, p)} \end{array}\right]$$

Vic's search will only be successful, if s/he encounters a record (a situation) that contains an individual of the type expressed by the record type p.

6 Conclusion

We presented QuantRTT, an annotation schema for quantified noun phrases based on RTT (Lücking and Ginzburg, 2022). The conceptual underpinnings have been introduced and used to derive the abstract syntax of the annotation schema. We see it as an advantage that QuantRTT brings about a cleaner separation of quantification and verbal predication. Furthermore, given the transparent noun phrase anatomy, QuantRTT arguably lends itself to the integration with anaphora annotation projects (e.g., Loáiciga et al., 2021), contributing to the interoperability of annotations. This could involve to include q-persp in annotations to account for QNPs and compset anaphora in a more systematic way.

A couple of examples comparing QuantML and QuantRTT have been discussed. Although the examples are typeset in the form of concrete XML syntax, there is no standard for QuantRTT yet. To make QuantRTT operable, two further, not mutually exclusive, steps are envisaged. Firstly, QuantRTT can be implemented as an "add-on" to QuantML, for instance as a plug-in as proposed for extensions to dialogue act annotation (Bunt, 2019a). This move will have benefits on both sides: QuantML is connected to RTT and phenomena not yet covered by RTT can be captured by appropriate QuantML resources (although it remains to be seen how well both approaches interact "out of the box"). Note in this context that the intersection of elements in the syntactic inventories of QuantML and QuantRTT is empty, meaning that they can in principle be annotated in parallel.

Secondly, QuantRTT will be incorporated in the TEXTANNOTATOR (Abrami et al., 2021), an annotation suite hosting several annotation tools. This move enables to make use of annotation support from automatic natural language pre-processing tools. Furthermore, due to the graphical user interface, the linking structure of dependent noun phrases can be added in a graphical display by drawing connecting edges.

Of course, QuantRTT will develop as RTT will – a few pointers into potential research directions (e.g., mass nouns and quantificational adverbials) have been given.

Acknowledgment

This work is partially supported by the *Deutsche Forschungsgemeinschaft* (DFG) [grant number LU 2114/2-1], and by a public grant overseen by the French National Research Agency (ANR) as part of the program "Investissements d'Avenir" (reference: ANR-10-LABX-0083). It contributes to the IdEx Université Paris Cité – ANR-18-IDEX-0001.

References

Giuseppe Abrami, Alexander Henlein, Andy Lücking, Attila Kett, Pascal Adeberg, and Alexander Mehler. 2021. Unleashing annotations with TextAnnotator: Multimedia, multi-perspective document views for ubiquitous annotation. In *Proceedings of the 17th Joint ACL–ISO Workshop on Interoperable Semantic Annotation*, pages 65–75, Groningen, The Netherlands (online). Association for Computational Linguistics.

Jon Barwise and Robin Cooper. 1981. Generalized quantifiers and natural language. *Linguistics and Philosophy*, 4(2):159–219.

Filippo Beghelli and Tim Stowell. 1997. Distributivity and negation: The syntax of *Each* and *Every*. In Anna Szabolcsi, editor, *Ways of Scope Taking*, Studies in Linguistics and Philosophy, chapter 3, pages 71–107. Kluwer Academic Publishers, Dordrecht, The Netherlands.

Harry Bunt. 2019a. Plug-ins for content annotation of dialogue acts. In *Proceedings of the Fifteenth Joint ACL-ISO Workshop on Interoperable Semantic Annotation*, ISA-15, pages 33–45.

Harry Bunt. 2019b. A semantic annotation scheme for quantification. In *Proceedings of the 13th International Conference on Computational Semantics – Long Papers*, pages 31–42. Association for Computational Linguistics.

Harry Bunt. 2020. Annotation of quantification: The current state of ISO 24617-12. In *Proceedings of the 16th Joint ACL-ISO Workshop Interoperable Semantic Annotation*, ISA-16, pages 1–12. European Language Resources Association (ELRA).

Harry Bunt, Maxime Amblard, Johan Bos, Karën Fort, Bruno Guillaume, Philippe de Groote, Chuyuan Li, Pierre Ludmann, Michel Musiol, Siyana Pavlova, Guy Perrier, and Sylvain Pogodalla. 2022. Quantification annotation in ISO 24617-12, second draft. In *Proceedings of the Thirteenth Language Resources and Evaluation Conference*, LREC'22, pages 3407–3416. European Language Resources Association.

Robin Cooper. 2005. Austinian truth, attitudes and type theory. *Research on Language and Computation*, 3(2-3):333–362.

Robin Cooper. 2008. Type theory with records and unification-based grammar. In Fritz Hamm and Stephan Kepser, editors, *Logics for Linguistic Structures*, number 201 in Trends in Linguistics: Studies and Monographs, pages 9–33. Mouton de Gruyter, Berlin and New York.

Robin Cooper. 2013. Clarification and generalized quantifiers. *Dialogue & Discourse*, 4(1):1–25.

Robin Cooper. 2023. *From Perception to Communication*. Oxford University Press, Oxford, UK.

Robin Cooper and Jonathan Ginzburg. 2015. Type theory with records for natural language semantics. In Shalom Lappin and Chris Fox, editors, *The Handbook of Contemporary Semantic Theory*, 2 edition, chapter 12, pages 375–407. Wiley-Blackwell, Oxford, UK.

Donald Davidson. 1967. The logical form of action sentences. In Nicholas Rescher, editor, *The Logic of Decision and Action*, pages 81–95. University of Pittsburgh Press, Pittsburgh.

Sara Del Negro. 2020. Komplementanaphern im Deutschen. Master's thesis, Karl-Franzens-Universität Graz.

Tim Fernando. 2007. Observing events and situations in time. *Linguistics and Philosophy*, 30:527–550.

Jonathan Ginzburg. 2012. *The Interactive Stance: Meaning for Conversation*. Oxford University Press, Oxford, UK.

Jonathan Ginzburg and Matthew Purver. 2012. Quantification, the reprise content hypothesis, and type theory. In Lars Borin and Staffan Larsson, editors, *From Quantification to Conversation. Festschrift for Robin Cooper on the occasion of his 65th birthday*. College Publications, London.

Hans Kamp and Uwe Reyle. 1993. *From Discourse to Logic*. Kluwer Academic Publishers, Dordrecht.

Edward L. Keenan and Jonathan Stavi. 1986. A semantic characterization of natural language determiners. *Linguistics and Philosophy*, 9(3):253–326.

Sharid Loáiciga, Simon Dobnik, and David Schlangen. 2021. Annotating anaphoric phenomena in situated dialogue. In *Proceedings of the 1st Workshop on Multimodal Semantic Representations*, MMSR, pages 78–88. Association for Computational Linguistics.

Andy Lücking. 2022. *Aspects of Multimodal Communication*. Habilitation, Université Paris Cité.

Andy Lücking and Jonathan Ginzburg. 2019. Not few but all quantifiers can be negated: Towards a referentially transparent semantics of quantified noun phrases. In *Proceedings of the Amsterdam Colloquium 2019*, AC'19, pages 269–278.

Andy Lücking and Jonathan Ginzburg. 2022. Referential transparency as the proper treatment of quantification. *Semantics and Pragmatics*, 15(4).

Andy Lücking, Jonathan Ginzburg, and Robin Cooper. 2021. Grammar in dialogue. In Stefan Müller, Anne Abeillé, Robert D. Borsley, and Jean-Pierre Koenig, editors, *Head Driven Phrase Structure Grammar: The handbook*, number 9 in Empirically Oriented Theoretical Morphology and Syntax, chapter 26, pages 1155–1199. Language Science Press, Berlin.

Per Martin-Löf. 1984. *Intuitionistic Type Theory*. Studies in Proof Theory. Bibliopolis, Napoli.

Rick Nouwen. 2003. Complement anaphora and interpretation. *Journal of Semantics*, 20(1):73–113.

Terence Parsons. 1990. *Events in the Semantics of English*. Number 19 in Current Studies in Linguistics Series. MIT Press, Cambridge.

Lance J. Rips and Susan J. Hespos. 2015. Divisions of the physical world: Concepts of objects and substances. *Psychological Bulletin*, 141(4):786–811.

Mats Rooth. 2016. Alternative semantics. In Caroline Féry and Shinichiro Ishihara, editors, *The Oxford Handbook of Information Structure*, chapter 2, pages 19–40. Oxford University Press, Oxford, UK.

Remko Scha. 1984. Distributive, collective and cumulative quantification. In Jeroen Groenendijk, Theo M. V. Janssen, and Martin Stokhof, editors, *Truth, Interpretation and Information: Selected Papers from the Third Amsterdam Colloquium*, number 2 in Groningen-Amsterdam Studies in Semantics, pages 131–158. de Gruyter Mouton.

Dag Westerståhl. 1985. Determiners and context sets. In Alice ter Meulen and Johan van Benthem, editors, *Generalized Quantifiers in Natural Language*, number 4 in Groningen-Amsterdam Studies in Semantics, pages 45–72. De Gruyter Mouton, Berlin.

Henk Zeevat. 2018. Interpreting dependent NPs. Talk given at *Cognitive Structures: Linguistic, Philosophical and Psychological Perspectives* (CoSt'18), Düsseldorf, Germany.

The compositional semantics of QuantML annotations

Harry Bunt
Department of Cognitive Science and Artificial Intelligence
School of Humanities and Digital Sciences
Tilburg University, Tilburg, Netherlands
harry.bunt@tilburguniversity.edu

Abstract

This paper discusses some issues in the semantic annotation of quantification phenomena in general, and in particular in the markup language QuantML, which has been proposed to form part of an ISO standard annotation scheme for quantification in natural language data. QuantML annotations have been claimed to have a compositional semantic interpretation, but the formal specification of QuantML in the official ISO documentation does not provide sufficient detail to judge this. This paper aims to fill this gap.

1 Introduction

The semantic annotation of quantification in natural language aims to enrich language data with information about the intended interpretation of the quantifications. The formulation of such annotations and their assignment to the data are challenging tasks, in view of the complexity of quantification phenomena in natural language. The many aspects of quantification, such as the distributivity, determinacy, countability, exhaustiveness, polarity and scope, make quantifications a major source of ambiguity and difficulty in computational semantics.

One of the challenges that quantifications pose for semantic annotation and representation is that, although much of the information about quantification is located in noun phrases, there may also be quantification information floating around in the form of adverbials, or encoded in language-specific morphosyntactic structure, or expressed by prosodic features (stress, pauses) (*"You heard a dog barking?" "TWO dogs barked."*) or typographical elements (use of capitals, underlining, punctuation). Semantic annotation faces the challenge of picking up these various pieces of information and assembling them in a useful form. The QuantML language is a proposal for such a form.

Another, fundamental challenge for quantification analysis concerns the choice of depth and detail, or 'granularity'. Studies of quantification phenomena in natural language have both benefited and suffered from studies of quantification in logic (Aristotle, 350 BC; Montague, 1971). The benefits are in the deep understanding of formal properties of and fine-grained distinctions between various types of quantification, which have contributed greatly to the emergence of the theory of generalized quantifiers (GQT, Barwise & Cooper, 1981). On the negative side, logic-based approaches tend to have weaknesses from an empirical linguistic point of view, since the fine-grained distinctions that can be expressed in formal logic tend to carry over to semantic representations of natural language expressions, while speakers and listeners are often unaware of these fine distinctions, thus creating a sort of artificial ambiguities. At this point semantic annotations may come in useful. A semantic annotation can be regarded as expressing constraints on the meaning of certain language data, without having the ambition of providing full-blown semantic representations, viz. to express 'the meaning' of the data. Annotations, by contrast, may express fewer or more, weaker or stronger constraints on interpretation. Still, in a context where high-precision interpretations are required, a semantic annotation scheme should allow detailed information to be captured by the annotations.

The present stage of defining an ISO standard annotation scheme for quantification, involving QuantML is documented in ISO CD 24617-12 (2023)(see Bunt et al. 2022). It follows the general principles for semantic annotation laid down in ISO 24617-5, Principles of Semantic Annotation (2015)(see also Bunt, 2016). One of these principles is that semantic annotations must have a well-defined semantics. In view of the challenges mentioned above, this means for QuantML the re-

Proceedings of the 19th Joint ACL - ISO Workshop on Interoperable Semantic Annotation, pages 56–65
June 20, 2023. ©2023 Association for Computational Linguistics

quirement to be flexible in the level of detail of its expressions, while having a semantics for its annotation structures, regardless the level of detail. The specification of QuantML in the ISO document goes a long way in this direction, outlining a compositional semantics of annotation structures, but this is not fully worked out for some of its structures. The present paper aims to remedy this.

The paper is organised as follows. Section 2 summarises the approach taken in developing QuantML. Section 3 discusses the annotation of scope relations, distinguishing wider, equal, and dual scoping. The semantics of these relations is considered, and their role in combining information from pairs of quantifications. Section 3 generalizes the semantic interpretation of annotations of multiple scoped quantifiers. Section 4 briefly discusses the instruments available in QuantML for varying the level of granularity in annotations. Section 5 wraps up and closes the paper.

2 ISO 24617-12 and QuantML

Following the ISO principles of semantic annotation (ISO 24617-5, 2015), QuantML has a triple-layered definition, based on a metamodel. The three layers are (a) an abstract syntax, using n-tuples of concepts; (b) a reference representation format based on XML, with encoding- and decoding mappings to the abstract syntax; and (c) a semantics, in the form of a function I_Q which translates abstract annotation structures into DRSs in a compositional way. The fact that the semantics is defined for the *abstract* syntax makes it possible to accommodate alternative representation formats, while preserving the meaning. An example of the abstract and concrete syntax of a QuantML annotation is given in (1).

(1) At least three students called more than once.

a. Markables: m_1 = "At least three", m_2 = "At least three students", m_3 = "students", m_4 = "called m_4 = "more than once", m_5 = "more than once"

b. Abstract syntax:
$L_1 = \langle \epsilon_e, \epsilon_{P1}$,Agent, individual, narrow$\rangle$, where:
$\epsilon_e = \langle m_4, \langle$call, $\langle >, 1\rangle\rangle\rangle$, and
$\epsilon_{P1} = \langle m_2, \langle$student, indeterminate$\rangle$, count, $\langle \geq, 3\rangle\rangle$

c. Concrete syntax:

```
<entity xml:id="x1 target="#m2" domain="#x2"
  involvement="n1" definiteness=indet/>
<refDomain xml:id="x2" target="#m3"
  source="#x3"/>
<cardinality xml:id="n1" target="m1" num-
  Rel="greaterthan" num="2">
<sourceDomain xml:id="x3" target="#m3" indivi-
  duation="count" pred="student"/>
<event xml:id="e1" target="#m4" pred="call"
  rep="#n2">
<cardinality xml:id="n2" target="m1" num-
  Rel="greaterthan" num="1">
<participation event="#e1" participant="#x1" sem-
  Role="agent" distr="individual"
  evScope ="narrow" />
```

Theoretically, QuantML is inspired mainly by GQT, by event semantics (Davidson, 1967; Parsons, 1990), and by Discourse Representation Theory (DRT, Kamp & Reyle 1993). Quantifiers are thus interpreted as properties of sets of individuals, typically expressed by noun phrases, which play certain semantic roles as participants in sets of events. This is reflected in the metamodel in Fig. 1, where participant sets, event sets, and the relation between them play center stage. The use of DRT is primarily motivated by the consideration that other parts of the ISO Semantic Annotation Framework also make use of DRT; otherwise, second-order logic would be equally well suitable.

3 Annotation Semantics

3.1 Basic Concepts and Metamodel

The semantic information that is captured by QuantML annotations is concentrated primarily in the specification of participant sets and their relation to event sets through participation links. The annotation describing a participant set contains local semantic information about the entities that populate the set; a participation link structure specifies properties of the relation between a participant set and the events in which they are involved. This includes information about the relative scopes of the quantification over participants and the quantification over events (the 'event scope').

Semantic information which is less local in character concerns the relative scoping of quantifications over participant sets involved with different semantic roles. The main challenge of a compositional interpretation of annotation structures is to combine the local semantic information in the participant sets and the participation link structures into a single semantic representation. The relative scoping of quantifiers has been studied extensively in formal logic and in formal and computational semantics in terms of wide and narrow scope (e.g. Hobbs & Shieber, 1987; Montague, 1974; Kamp & Reyle, 1983: Szabolcsi, 2010), mostly for count nouns and for distributive readings. With these limitations, the semantics of quantification annotations would be fairly straightforward.

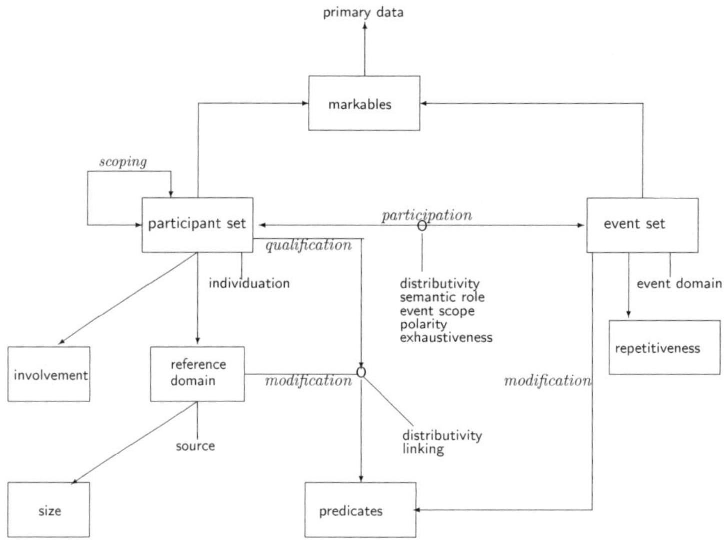

Figure 1: QuantML metamodel.

Besides distributive readings, also collective readings display scope ambiguities. A set of participants that is involved collectively in certain events might appear to be acting as a single entity, and the notion of scope would therefore not apply. However, consider the sentences in (2):

(2) a. The two men moved all the pianos.
All the pianos were moved by the two men.
b. All the pianos were moved by two men.
c. Two men moved all the pianos.

Both sentences in (a) can only be read as saying that the same two men moved all the pianos, giving the quantification over men wider scope than the one over pianos. Sentence (b), by contrast, has the preferred reading where the various pianos were moved by pairs of men, but not necessarily all by the same pair, and thus having the inverse scoping. Sentence (2c) has both readings. So clearly, issues of scope do apply also in the case of quantifications with collective distributivity.

3.2 Abstract syntax and semantics

Since the semantic contributions of the participant and event structures are included in the participation link structure, the semantic interpretation of the annotation of the sentence is just the interpretation of the participation link structures. More generally, the abstract syntax of the QuantML annotation for a sentence with two or more quantifiers (as expressed by NPs) is the collection of participation link structures plus the collection of scope relations between them, and the semantic interpretation of the annotation structure is obtained by combining the semantics of the individual participation structures in a way determined by the scope relations.

4 Scope relations in QuantML

4.1 Scoping and 'plint structures'

In QuantML three scope relations among participation link structures are distinguished:

1. Wider: one quantification outscopes the other. Example: "Every student speaks two languages" (but not necessarily the same two). The DRSs representing the semantics of the participation links are combined by means of an operation called *'scoped merge'*.

2. Dual: two quantifications mutually outscope each other (so-called 'cumulative' quantification). Example: "Three breweries supplied more than 5000 inns". The corresponding DRSs are combined by means of an operation called *'dual-scoped merge'*.

3. Equal: two quantifications have equal scope (so-called 'cluster' or 'group' quantification). Example: "Seven boys played against eleven girls", in the sense of teams of seven boys playing against teams of eleven girls. The corresponding DRSs are combined by means of the standard DRS-merge.

The semantics of the scope links determines how the participation link interpretation structures, or *'plint structures'*, should be combined. This is expressed in (3).

(3) For any scope relation s, if $L'_i =_D I_Q(L_i)$:
$I_Q(L_1, L_2, s) = I_Q(s)(L'_1, L'_2)$

The scope relation between two quantifications is semantically interpreted as an operation on two plint structures, using the standard DRS-merge and two scope-dependent forms of merge, called *scoped merge* ($\cup^*$) and *dual-scoped merge* ($\cup^{\otimes}$). These operations are defined below.

(4) I_Q(wider) = $\lambda x.\lambda y.x \cup^* y$;
I_Q(equal) = $\lambda x.\lambda y.x \cup y$;
I_Q(dual) = $\lambda x.\lambda y.x \cup^{\otimes} y$

The semantics of each of the scope relations is discussed in subsequent subsections.

4.2 Wider scope

The scoped merge operator $\cup^*$ takes two plint structures L'_1 and L'_2 as arguments and merges them into a single DRS. Since the L_1-quantification has scope over the L_2-quantification, the DRS that represents the latter quantification is moved into the DRS that represents the L_1-quantification, in such a way that it falls within the scope of that quantification. Moreover, since the two plint structures link participant sets to the same set of events, the two event quantifications are collapsed into one. In terms of DRS merging this means that a discourse referent is introduced which refers to the event set, in a position determined by the two event scopes, [1] and the nuclear content of L'_1 is added to the nucleus of the L'_2 - quantification. This expressed in (5).

(5) **Scoped merge.**
Given two plint structures L'_1 and L'_2, the scoped merge moves L_2' as a sub-DRS into the DRS L'_1, bringing the L'_2-quantification within the scope of the L'_1-quantification and merging the event quantifications.

The formal definition of the scoped merge is formulated in terms of pattern-matching based operations, since the structures that it applies to have certain specific structural properties. Every plint structure contains three parts:

(6) 1. the introduction of a participant set, i.e. a DRS of the form $[X|C_1, x \in X \rightarrow K_1(x)]$, where the discourse referent X refers to the participant set, C_1 is a set of conditions, and the sub-DRS K_1 represents the quantifying predicate;
2. the introduction of an event set, a DRS of the form $[E|C_e, e \in E \rightarrow K_2(e)]$;
3. the nucleus, a sub-DRS of the form $R_i(e, x)$, where the semantic role R_i relates events and participants.

A plint structure where the second part constitutes the K_1 subexpression of the first part represents a quantification with narrow event scope; one where the first part constitutes the K_2 subexpression of the second part represents wide event scope. Schematically, these two forms of a plint structure have the top-level structures shown in (7)

(7) a. $[X_i|C_i, x \in X_i \rightarrow K_i(x)]$, with
$K_1 = \lambda z.[E|C_e, e \in E \rightarrow R_i(e, z)]$

b. $[E|C_e, e \in E \rightarrow K_i(e)]$, with
$K_1 = \lambda u.[X_i|C_i, x \in X_i \rightarrow R_i(u, z)]$

Both forms come in two variants, depending on the distributivity of the quantification with individual or unspecific distributivity. In the individual case, the elements of the participant set are involved individually; in the unspecific case also as subsets. This leads to differences in K_1 and K_2 in (6). In the case of collective quantification we see a first part of the form $[X|C_1, K_1(X)]$ rather than $[X|C_1, x \in X \rightarrow K_1(x)]$, for narrow-scope interpretations and $[X, E|C_1, C_e, e \in E \rightarrow K_2(e, X)]$ in case of wide event scope,. The six possible forms of plint structures for all combinations of event scope and distributivity (and positive polarity and non-exhaustive, see below) are listed in (8).

(8) a. Narrow event scope, individual distributivity: $[X|\mathrm{C}_i, x \in X \rightarrow [E|\mathrm{C}_e, e \in E \rightarrow R(e, x)]]$ or, schematically, with K as in (7a): $[X|C, x \in X \rightarrow K(x)]$

b. Wide event scope, individual distributivity: $[E|C_e, e \in E \rightarrow [XC_i, x \in X \rightarrow R(e, x)]]$ or, schematically, with K as in (7b): $[E|C_e, e \in E \rightarrow K(e)]$

c. Narrow event scope, collective distributivity: $[E, X|C, C_e, e \in E \rightarrow R(e, X)]]$ or, schematically, with $K = \lambda z.R(e, z)$: $[E, X|C, C_e, e \in E \rightarrow K(e, X)]$

[1] More precisely, the quantification over events is in the position with most narrow scope which is consistent with the event scopes.

d. Wide event scope, collective distributivity:
$[E|C_e, e \in E \rightarrow [X|C, R(e,X)]]$
or, schematically:
$[E|C_e, e \in E \rightarrow K(e,X)]$,
with $K = \lambda u.[X|x \in X \rightarrow R(u,X)$

e. Narrow event scope, unspecific distributivity, where $X^* =_D X \cup \mathcal{P}(X)$:
$[X|C, x \in X \rightarrow [E|C_e, e \in E \rightarrow$
$[y \in X^*|x = y \vee x \in y, R_i(e,y)]]]$,
schematically: $[X|C, x \in X \rightarrow K(x]$,
$K = \lambda z.[E|C_e, e \in E \rightarrow$
$[y| \in X^*, ...R(e,y)$

f. Wide event scope, unspecific distributivity:
$[E|C_e, e \in E \rightarrow [X|C, x \in X \rightarrow$
$[y \in X^*|x = y \vee x \in y, R(e,y)]]]]$,
schematically, with K similar to case e:
$[E|C_e, e \in E \rightarrow K(e)]$.

In sum, plint structures can have the following schematic forms:

(9) a. $[X_i|C_i, x \in X_i \rightarrow K_i(x)]$
b. $[E|C_e, e \in E \rightarrow K_i(e)]$
c. $[E, X_i|C_i, C_e, e \in E \rightarrow K_i(e, X_i)]$

The scoped merge of two plint structures L'_1 and L'_2, where the first has wider scope than the second, combines the content of the two structures in a way that depends on their schematic forms. This is indicated in Table 1, where the '∪' indicator means that the scoped merge in this case is just the standard DRS-merge; the indicators 'A', 'B', and 'C' are defined in (10).

	a, e	b, d, f	c
a, e	A	B	B
b, f	–	C	–
c	–	∪	∪

Table 1: Scoped merge as depending on schematic argument structures

(10) Indicators used in Table 1:
∪: $L'_1 \cup L'_2$
A: $[X_1|C_1, x{\in}X_1 \rightarrow [X_2|C_2, y \in X_2 \rightarrow (K_1(x) \cup K_2(y))]]$
B: $[X_1|C_1, x{\in}X_1 \rightarrow (K_1(x) \cup L'_2)]$
C: $[E|C_e, e \in E \rightarrow [X_1|C_1, x \in X_1 \rightarrow$
$[X_2|y \in X_2 \rightarrow N_1(e,x) \cup N_2(e,y)]]]$,
where N_i is $\lambda z.\lambda u.R_i(u,z)$

Note that Table 1 indicates that the scoped merge is undefined for certain combinations of argument forms. This is because in those cases the relative scopes are inconsistent with the event scopes of the arguments. See Section 5.3. An example of applying the scoped merge is shown in (11).

(11) Some students read more than three papers.

a. Markables: m_1 = "Some students", m_2 = "students", m_3 = "read", m_4 = "more than three", m_5 = "more than three papers", m_6 = "papers"

b. QuantML annotation, XML-based concrete syntax:

```
<entity xml:id="x1" target="#m2" domain="#x2"
  involvement="some" definiteness=indet/>
<refDomain xml:id="x2" target="#m3"
  source="#x3"/>
<sourceDomain xml:id="x3" target="#m3"
  individuation="count" pred="student"/>
<event xml:id="e1" target="#m4" pred="read">
<participation event="#e1" participant="#x1" sem-
  Role="agent" distr="individual"
  evScope ="narrow" />
<entity xml:id="x4" target="#m5" domain="#x5"
  involvement="n1" definiteness=indet/>
<refDomain xml:id="x5" target="#m6"
  source="#x6"/>
<sourceDomain xml:id="x6" target="#m6"
  Rel="greaterthan" num="3">
<participation event="#e1" participant="#x4" sem-
  Role="theme" distr="individual"
  evScope ="narrow" />
<scoping arg1="#x1" arg2='#x4"
  scopeRel ="wider" />
```

c. QuantML annotation, abstract syntax:
$L_1 = \langle \epsilon_e, \epsilon_{P1}$,Agent, individual, narrow$\rangle$,
$L_2 = \langle \epsilon_e, \epsilon_{P2}$Theme, individual, narrow$\rangle$, where
$\epsilon_e = \langle m_4, \langle \text{read} \rangle \rangle$,
ϵ_{P1}=$\langle m_2$, $\langle$student, indeterminate$\rangle$, count, some $\rangle$,
$\epsilon_{P2} = \langle m_2$, $\langle$paper, indeterminate$\rangle$, count, $\langle \geq, 4 \rangle \rangle$
Scoping;
$sc_1 = \langle L'_1, L'_2$, wider $\rangle$

d. Semantics:
$L'_1 = [X_1|X_1 \subseteq \text{student}, x \in X_1 \rightarrow [E|E \subseteq \text{read}]$
$e \in E \rightarrow \text{agent}(e,x)]]$,
$L'_2 = [X_2|X_2 \subseteq \text{paper}, X_2| > 3, y \in X_2 \rightarrow$
$[E|E \subseteq \text{read}, e \in E \rightarrow \text{theme}(e,y)]]$,
$L'_1 \cup^* L'_2 = [X_1|X_1 \subseteq \text{student}, x \in X_1 \rightarrow$
$[X_2|X_2 \subseteq \text{paper}, y \in X_2 \rightarrow$
$[E|E \subseteq \text{read} \mid e \in E \rightarrow$
$[\,\text{agent}(e,x), \text{theme}(e,y)]]]$

In addition to the possible forms of the DRSs that interpret a participation structure with positive polarity, listed in (8), slightly different forms represent the semantics of negative-polarity quantifications. A participation link structure with wide-scope negative polarity corresponds to one the plint structures of (8) with an additional top-level negation; one with narrow-scope negative polarity and narrow event scope (cases (8a) and (8f)) have a negated sub-DRS that introduces the event set, which does not alter the schematic structure.

The scoped merge is defined only for two plint structures with the same polarity, with the following effects if both arguments have negative polarity.

(12) a. If both arguments have wide-scope negative polarity, then their scoped merge is as defined in (10), with the resulting DRS being negated.

b. If both arguments have narrow-scope negative polarity, then their scoped merge is exactly as defined in (10), since the negations are incorporated in sub-DRSs of the two arguments that represent the quantification over the event set.

Another complication for plint structures is due to the possible internal complexity of a participant set specification. As the metamodel in Fig. 1 indicates, a participant set may have 'qualifications', i.e. one or more specifications of non-restrictive modifications ('appositives'); moreover, the reference domain of which it is a subset may have an (absolute or relative) size specification, and may be co-determined by restrictive modifications (which come with their own distributivity and scope linking).

The plint structures listed in (8) all introduce a discourse referent used to refer to a participant set (indicated by 'X_i') and include a set of conditions 'C_i' that contains a restriction like $x \in X_i \rightarrow$ student(x), stipulating that the participant set is a set of students. This is adequate for simple quantifiers like *"some students"* and *"five students"*, but it is not expressive enough for quantifiers like *"three of the four eggs"*, in example (13). The cardinal determiner *"three"* in this example indicates the size of the participant set ('involvement' in Fig. 1), while *"four"* indicates the size of the reference domain. To accommodate this, a second discourse referent is introduced that refers to the reference domain, indicated in (13) byX', where the indexed predicate 'egg$_0$' is used to indicate the predicate 'egg' (denoting the source domain of all eggs) restricted to its contextually relevant subset.

(13) a. Three of the four eggs have hatched.

b. $[X, X'|C_1, x \in X \rightarrow [E|e \in E \rightarrow$ $[\,\text{hatch}(e), \text{theme}(e,x)\,]]]$, with $C_1 = \{|X| = 3, |X'| = 4, X \subseteq X',$ $y \in X' \leftrightarrow \text{egg}_0(y)\}$

This addition does not alter the schematic form of the plint structure, apart from the introduction of a second discourse referent. This additional element does not play an active role in the scoped merge; it is merely dragged along when plint structures are combined. This possible complication is therefore disregarded in the rest of this paper.

4.3 Dual scope

The 'dual' scope relation is used in QuantML for the annotation of cases of cumulative quantification. Cumulative quantification may occur in sentences with two numerical determiners (Krifka, 1999) as in the most plausible reading of example sentence (14), due to Reyle (1983).

(14) Three breweries supplied twelvehundred inns.

In the cumulative interpretation, none of the two quantifiers has wider scope than the other; rather, it says that each one of a set of three breweries supplied some of 1200 inns, and vice versa. In QuantML, this is analysed as mutual outscoping: the quantification over breweries has wider scope than the one over inns, and vice versa.

The semantics of a dual-scope relation involves the use of an operation similar to the scoped merge operation, called *dual-scoped merge* and symbolised by $\cup^{\otimes}$. The operation is used for combining two plint structures for non-collective quantification with narrow event scope and positive polarity. Quantifications with collective distributivity, wide event scope, or negative polarity do not allow cumulative interpretations, hence only plint structures of the form (8) (a) or (e) are involved. The dual-scoped merge is defined as follows.

(15) **Dual-scoped merge.**
The dual-scoped merge combines two plint structures L_1', L_2' into a DRS that inherits the discourse referents of both arguments, and branches out into two sub-DRSs, corresponding to the two sides of mutual outscoping, which both have the merge of the L_1' and L_2' nuclei as their nucleus.

To express this in formal terms, note that the operation is defined as applicable only to plint structures of the form of (8a) or (8e), which both have the schematic form $[X_i|C_i, x \in X_i \rightarrow K_i(x)]$ (see (9a)). Applying the dual-scoped merge to two arguments of this form is the following operation on plint structures:

(16) $L_1' \cup^{\otimes} L_2' = [X_1, X_2|C_1, C_2,$ $x_1 \in X_1 \rightarrow [x_2|x_2 \in X_2, K_1 \cup K_2],$ $x_2 \in X_2 \rightarrow [x_1|x_1 \in X_1, K_1 \cup K_2]]$

As an example, consider the sentence in (14). The abstract syntax of the QuantML annotation of this sentence would include two plint structures of the same form as those in (11). Application of the dual-scoped merge gives the following result:

(17) $[X_1, X_2 | X_1 \subseteq \text{brewery}, |X_1| = 3,$
$x_1 \in X_1 \rightarrow [x_2 \in X_2 \rightarrow E \subseteq \text{supply}|$
$[\text{agent}(e, x_1), \text{beneficiary}(e, x_2)]],$
$x_2 \in X_2 \rightarrow [x_1 \in X_1 \rightarrow E \subseteq \text{supply}|$
$[\text{agent}(e, x_1), \text{beneficiary}(e, x_2)]]]$

4.4 Equal scope

The equal scope relation is used specifically for cases of cluster quantification (or 'group quantification'), as mentioned in Section 4.1. The semantics of an "equal" scope annotation is defined through application of the standard DRS-merge. For example, the QuantML annotation of the sentence (18a) is as follows.

(18) Seven boys played against eleven girls.

a. Markables: m_1 = "Seven boys", m_2 = "boy", m_3 = "played against", m_4 = "eleven girls", m_5 = "girls"

b. QuantML annotation, XML-based concrete syntax:

```
<entity xml:id="x1" target="#m1" indiv="count", domain="#x2",
   involvement="7" determinacy=indet/>
<refDomain xml:id="x2" target="#m3"
   source="#x3"/>
<sourceDomain   xml:id="x3"   target="#m2" pred="boy"
<event xml:id="e1" target="#m4" pred="play">
<participation event="#e1" participant="#x1" semRole="agent" distr="individual"
   evScope ="wide" />
<entity xml:id="x4" target="#m4" domain="#x5"
   involvement="11" determinacy=indet/>
<refDomain xml:id="x5" target="#m6"
   source="#x6"/>
<sourceDomain xml:id="x6" target="#m5"
<participation event="#e1" participant="#x4" semRole="theme" distr="individual"
   evScope ="idew" />
<scoping arg1="#x1" arg2='#x4"
   scopeRel ="equal" />
```

c. QuantML annotation, abstract syntax:
$L_1 = \langle \epsilon_e, \epsilon_{P1}, \text{Agent, individual, wide} \rangle$,
$L_2 = \langle \epsilon_e, \epsilon_{P2} \text{ Agent, individual, wide} \rangle$, where
$\epsilon_e = \langle \text{m}_4, \langle \text{play} \rangle \rangle$,
$\epsilon_{P1} = \langle \text{m}_2, \langle \text{boy, 7, indeterminate} \rangle, \text{count, some} \rangle$,
$\epsilon_{P2} = \langle \text{m}_2, \langle \text{girl,11, indeterminate} \rangle, \text{count}, \langle \geq, 4 \rangle \rangle$
Scoping;
$sc_1 = \langle L'_1, L'_2, \text{equal} \rangle$

d. Semantics:
$L'_1 = [E | E \subseteq \text{play}, e \in E \rightarrow [X | X \subseteq \text{boy},$
$|X| = 7, \text{agent}(e, xX]]$
$L'_2 = [E | E \subseteq \text{play}, e \in E \rightarrow [Y | Y \subseteq \text{girl},$
$|Y| = 11, \text{agent}(e, Y)]],$
$L'_1 \cup L'_2 = [E \subseteq \text{play} \mid e \in E \rightarrow [X | X \subseteq \text{boy},$
$Y \subseteq \text{girl}, |X| = 7|, |Y| = 11,$
$[\text{agent}(e, X), \text{agent}(e, Y)]]]$

5 Clause-level annotation structures

5.1 Scoping multiple quantifiers

The semantics of the QuantML annotation of a clause with two scoped quantifications is defined by (3) and (4) plus the definitions of the scoped merge and the dual-scoped merge. For clauses with more than two scoped quantifications, the definitions of the scoped merge and the dual-scoped merge can be generalized so as to apply to more than two plint structures as arguments, or so as to apply to two arguments one of which is a plint structure and the other one a plint structure or the result of combining two ore more plint structures. In this section we take the latter approach, thus keeping all scope relations and merge operations binary.

The abstract syntax of a fully scoped clause annotation includes a number of binary scope relations of the form $\langle L_i, L_j, R \rangle$, where $R \in \{\text{wider, dual, equal}\}$. For example, if L_1, L_2, and L_3 are three participation links, of which L_1 has wider scope than L_2, while L_2 and L_3 have dual scope, then the semantics of their combination can be computed in two ways, shown in (19).

(19) a. $L'_1 \cup^* (L'_2 \cup^{\otimes} L'_3)$

b. $(L'_1 \cup^* L'_2) \cup^{\otimes} L'_3)$

More generally, for a clause annotation which contains n participation links, $n-2$ of the links are involved in two scope relations, like $L_1 - L_2$ and $L_2 - L_3$ in the case of example (19). These links define a linked chain like $L_1 - L_2 - L_3$, of which the begin-and end points are the two links that are involved in only one scope relation. Following the approach of (19a), if $\sigma_{i,j}$ designates the scoping relation between L_i and L_j, and $\sigma'_{i,j} = I_Q(\sigma_{i,j})$, the interpretation of such a chain is defined by (20).

(20) $I_Q([L_1, L_2, .., L_n] =$
$L'_1 \; \sigma'_{1,2} \; (L'_2 \; \sigma'_{2,3} \; ... \; (L_{n-1} \; \sigma'_{n-1,n} \; L'_n)..)$

5.2 Generalized scoped merge

To implement the semantic interpretation of linked chains of scoped participation links, we generalise the scoped merge and the dual-scoped merge operations to apply to two arguments, the first of which is a plint structure and the second either a plint structure or a DRS constructed by applying one of the merge operations defined above or the standard DRS-merge. This comes down to allowing the second argument to be a DRS which has a sub-DRS that expresses a quantification over the same set of events as in the first argument, since both arguments are concerned with participation in the same set of events. The two event quantifications are merged into one, in order to take that into account.

(21) **Generalized scoped merge.**
Given a plint structure L_1' and a DRS A_2 which contains a sub-DRS expressing a quantification over the same events as in L_1', the generalised scoped merge inserts the DRS A_2 into L_1' immediately below the top level and merges the two event quantifications.

Example:

(22) Both candidates presented a view to the committee members.

a. Markables: m_1 = "All candidates", m_2 = "candidate", m_3 = "presented", m_4 = "a vision", m_5 = "a vision", m_6 = "vision", m_7 = "the committee members", m_8 = "committee members"

b. QuantML annotation, XML-based concrete syntax:

```
<entity xml:id="x1" target="#m2" domain="#x2"
  involvement="all" definiteness=det/>
<refDomain xml:id="x2" target="#m2"
  source="#x3"/>
<sourceDomain xml:id="x3" target="#m2"
  individuation="count" pred="candidate"/>
<event xml:id="e1" target="#m3" pred="present">
<participation event="#e1" participant="#x1" semRole="agent" distr="individual"
  evScope ="narrow" />
<entity xml:id="x4" target="#m4" domain="#x5"
  involvement="some" definiteness=indet/>
<refDomain xml:id="x5" target="#m6"
  source="#x6"/>
<sourceDomain xml:id="x6" target="#m6"
  individuation="count" pred="vision"/>
<participation event="#e1" participant="#x4" semRole="theme" distr="individual"
  evScope ="narrow" />
<entity xml:id="x7" target="#m7" domain="#x8"
  involvement="all" definiteness=det/>
<refDomain xml:id="x8" target="#m8"
  source="#x3"/>
<sourceDomain xml:id="x9" target="#m8"
  individuation="count" pred="committee-members"/>
<scoping arg1="#x1" arg2='#x4"
  scopeRel ="wider" />
<scoping arg1="#x4" arg2='#x7"
  scopeRel ="wider" />
```

c. QuantML annotation, abstract syntax:
$L_1 = \langle \epsilon_e, \epsilon_{P1}$,Agent, individual, narrow$\rangle$,
$L_2 = \langle \epsilon_e, \epsilon_{P2}$Theme, individual, narrow$\rangle$,
$L_1 = \langle \epsilon_e, \epsilon_{P1}$,Beneficiary, individual, narrow$\rangle$,
where
$\epsilon_e = \langle m_4, \langle \text{present} \rangle \rangle$,
$\epsilon_{P1} = \langle m_2, \langle \text{candidate, determinate} \rangle, \text{count, all} \rangle$,
$\epsilon_{P2} = \langle m_2, \langle \text{vision, indeterminate} \rangle, \text{count, some} \rangle$
$\epsilon_{P3} = \langle m_2, \langle \text{commember, determinate} \rangle, \text{count, all} \rangle$,
Scoping;
$sc_1 = \langle L_1', L_2', \text{wider} \rangle$, $sc_2 = \langle L_2', L_3', \text{wider} \rangle$

d. Semantics:
$L_1' = [X_1 \subseteq \text{candidate}_O \mid \text{candidate}_O \subseteq X_1,$
$x \in X_1 \to [E \subseteq \text{present} \mid e \in E \to$
$\text{agent}(e, x)]]$,
$L_2' = [X_2 \subseteq \text{vision} | y \in X_2 \to$
$[E \subseteq \text{present} \mid e \in E \to \text{theme}(e, y)]]$,
$L_3' = [X_3 \subseteq \text{commember}_O \mid \text{commember}_O \subseteq X_3,$
$z \in X_3 \to [E \subseteq \text{present} \mid e \in E \to$
$\text{beneficiary}(e, z)]]$
$L_1' \cup^* (L_2' \cup^* L_3') =$
$[X_1 \subseteq \text{candidate}_O \mid \text{candidate}_O \subseteq X_1,$
$x \in X_1 \to [X_2 \subseteq \text{vision}, y \in X_2 \to$
$[X_2 \subseteq \text{vision}, y \in X_2 \to$
$[X_3 \subseteq \text{commembers}, y \in X_2 \to$
$[E \subseteq \text{present} \mid e \in E \to$
$[\ \text{agent}(e, x), \text{theme}(e, y),$
$\text{beneficiary}(e, z)]]]]$

5.3 Generalized dual-scoped merge

The dual-scope merge can be generalized in a similar way. With the generalized scoped merge and dual-scoped merge (and the standard DRS-merge) we can compute the compositional semantic interpretation of any fully scoped collection of participation links, using (20) with $\sigma_{i,j} \in \{\cup^*, \cup^\otimes, U\}$. However, cumulative quantification, for which the dual-scoped merge is used, does not seem to make sense in combination with collective distributivity, wide event scope or negative polarity. The definition below therefore restricts its arguments to represent quantification annotations with individual or unspecific distribution, narrow event scope, and positive polariy.

(23) **Generalized dual-scoped merge.**
Given a plint structure L_1' for non-collective distributivity and narrow event scope and a DRS K that contains a sub-DRS expressing a quantification over the same events as in L_1', a DRS is formed that inherits the discourse referents of both arguments and branches out just below the top level into two sub-DRSs, corresponding to either of the two argument scopings, and in both of which the two event quantifications are merged.

A representative example of the use of the generalized dual-scoped merge is shown in (24).

(24) Each of these breweries sold over six hundred thousand casks of beer to five hundred inns.

$L_1' \cup^* (L_2' \cup^\otimes L_3') =$
$[X_1 \subseteq \text{brewery}_O, x \in X_1 \to$
$[X_2 \subseteq \text{cask}, X_3 \subseteq \text{inn} \mid y \in X_2 \to$
$[z \in X_3, E \subseteq \text{sell} \mid$

5.4 Event scope and participant scoping

Event scope, annotated in participation link structures, interacts with relative participant scoping; some combinations are inconsistent. Interestingly, such cases do not seem to occur in natural language. As an illustration, sentence (25b) does not seem to have a reading in which there was event in which all the inhabitants were killed (wide event scope), and for certain bomb fragments there were bombing events in which they caused inhabitants to die (narrow event scope).

(25) In the bombing, all the inhabitants were killed by bomb fragments.

Champollion (2015) claims that event scope is *always* narrow, which would mean that event scope does not need to be annotated at all and inconsistencies with relative scoping cannot occur. A sentence like *"Everybody died in the crash."* would seem to contradict this claim, however, as does (25).

6 Granularity in QuantML annotations

The preceding sections were inspired by the aim of allowing fine-grained annotation of quantification in a semantically well-defined way. As mentioned in Section 1, another important aim of semantic annotation is to allow representations which are *not* so fine-grained, since in many use contexts it is not relevant to make very fine-grained interpretations. This is especially true of quantifications, where issues of scope, distributivity, and exhaustiveness are not in all use cases of great interest. In this section we briefly consider the instruments that are available in QuantML for making annotations that are not maximally fine-grained.

First, QuantML annotations are modular. The abstract syntax of clause annotation structure contains a collection of entity structures and link structures When some of the components are missing, due to incomplete information, this and does not necessarily make the annotation structure uninterpretable, but allows it for example to be interpreted as an underspecified DRS (Reyle, 1993).

Second, some of the information in an annotation structure may be optional. Bunt et al. (2018) distinguish three types of optionality, which are all present in QuantML. *Semantic optionality* is that an annotation structure may have a certain component, according to its abstract syntax definition, but is also allowed without that component. Examples are the specification of the size of a reference domain and the specification of non-restrictive modifiers. Annotation structures with such components have a more specific semantics. *Syntactic optionality* is that a certain component does not need to be specified in annotation representations (using XML or some other format) but does have a default value in the encoded abstract syntax. Examples are the polarity and event scope of participation link structures. Finally, it may be convenient to allow certain components in concrete representations which do not encode anything in the abstract syntax, and thus have no semantic interpretation. Example are the marking up of a quantification as generic and, in ISO-TimeML (ISO 24617-1:2012) the encoding of parts of speech to distinguish verbal from nominal descriptions of events.

Third, some aspects of the information may be specified by more or less specific values. An example is the "unspecific" distributivity, which allows participant sets containing both individual objects and sets of individual objects. This is illustrated in plint structures of the form (8e) and(8f).

7 Concluding remarks

This paper presents certain details of the semantic definition of QuantML annotations that have so far been outlined only sketchily in the formal specification of QuantML (ISO CD 24617-12: 2023; see also Bunt, 2020). Various forms of merge operation on discourse representation structures, relying on pattern matching techniques, have been shown to allow for a compositional interpretation of annotation structures that describe quantifications in terms of sets of events and multiple sets of participants.

With the availability of the instruments mentioned in the previous section for avoiding being over-specific, QuantML aims to strike a balance between allowing fine-grained and more coarse-grained, empirically useful annotations of quantification phenomena, supported in all case by a compositional semantic interpretation.

Acknowledgements

I would like to thank Jae-Woong Choe, Robin Cooper, Rainer Osswald and Stephen Pulman for their comments on an earlier version of this paper.

References

Aristotle (350BC). *Analytika Protera. Translated into English as Prior Analytics by A.J. Jenkinson. Published by Kessinger Publishers (2010).*

Barwise, J. and R. Cooper (1981). Generalized Quantifiers and Natural Language. *Linguistics and Philosophy 4*, 159–219.

Bunt, H. (2015). On the principles of semantic annotation. In *Proceedings 11th Joint ACL-ISO Workshop on Interoperable Semantic Annotation (ISA-11)*, London, pp. 1–13.

Bunt, H. (2020). *Semantic Annotation of Quantification in Natural Language, Ed. 2. TiCC Technical Report* 2019-12. Tilburg Center for Cognition and Communication, Tilburg University.

Bunt, H., M. Amblard, J. .Bos, K.Fort, P. de Groote, B. Guillaume, C. Li, P. Ludmann, M. Musiol, G. Perrier, S. Pavlova, and S. Pogadalla (2022). Quantification Annotation in ISO 24617-12, second edition. In *Proceedings 13th International Conference on Language Resources and Evaluation (LREC 2022)*, Marselle, France.

Champollion, L. (2015). The interaction of compositional semantics and event semantics. *Linguistics and Philosophy 38 (1)*, 31–66.

Davidson, D. (1967). The Logical Form of Action Sentences. In N. Resher (Ed.), *The Logic of Decision and Action*, pp. 81–95. Pittsburgh: The University of Pittsburgh Press.

Hobbs, J. and S. Shieber (1987). An algorithm for generating quantifier scopings. *Computational Linguistics 13*(1-2), 47–63.

ISO (2015). *ISO 24617-6:2015, Language Resource Management - Semantic Annotation Framework (SemAF) - Part 6: Principles of semantic annotation.* Geneva: International Organisation for Standardisation ISO.

ISO (2022). *ISO/CD 24617-12:2022, Language Resource Management: Semantic Annotation Framework (SemAF) - Part 12: Quantification.* Geneva.: International Standard. International Organisation for Standardisation ISO.

Kamp, H. and U. Reyle (1993). *From Discourse to Logic*. Dordrecht: Kluwer Academic Publishers.

Krifka, M. (1999). At least some determiners aren't determiners. In K. Turner (Ed.), *The Semantics/Pragmatics Interface From Different Points of View*, pp. 257–291. Amsterdam: Elsevier.

Lee, K. (2023). *Annotation-based Semantics for Space and Time in Language.* Cambridge University Press.

Montague, R. (1971). The proper treatment of quantification in ordinary language. In R.Thomason (Ed.), *Formal Philosophy*. New Haven: Yale University Press.

Parsons, T. (1990). *Events in the Semantics of English: A Study in Subatomic Semantics.* Cambridge, MA: MIT Press.

Reyle, U. (1993). Dealing with ambiguities by underspecification: Construction, representation, and deduction. *Journal of Semantics*, 123–179.

Szabolcsi, A. (2010). *Quantification.* Cambridge (UK): Cambridge University Press.

An Abstract Specification of VoxML as an Annotation Language

Kiyong Lee
Dept. of Linguistics
Korea University, Seoul
ikiyong@gmail.com

Nikhil Krishnaswamy
Dept. of Computer Science
Colorado State University
nkrishna@colostate.edu

James Pustejovsky
Dept. of Computer Science
Brandeis University
jamesp@brandeis.edu

Abstract

VoxML is a modeling language used to map natural language expressions into real-time visualizations using commonsense semantic knowledge of objects and events. Its utility has been demonstrated in embodied simulation environments and in agent-object interactions in situated multimodal human-agent collaboration and communication. It introduces the notion of object affordance (both Gibsonian and Telic) from HRI and robotics, as well as the concept of habitat (an object's context of use) for interactions between a rational agent and an object. This paper aims to specify VoxML as an annotation language in general abstract terms. It then shows how it works on annotating linguistic data that express visually perceptible human-object interactions. The annotation structures thus generated will be interpreted against the enriched minimal model created by VoxML as a modeling language while supporting the modeling purposes of VoxML linguistically.

1 Introduction

As introduced by Pustejovsky and Krishnaswamy (2016), VoxML is a modeling language encoding the spatial and visual components of an object's conceptual structure.[1] It allows for 3D visual interpretations and simulations of objects, motions, and actions as minimal models from verbal descriptions. The data structure associated with this is called a *voxeme*, and the library of voxemes is referred to as a *voxicon*.

VoxML elements are conceptually grounded by a conventional inventory of semantic types (Pustejovsky, 1995; Pustejovsky and Batiukova, 2019). They are also enriched with a representation of how and when an object affords interaction with another object or an agent. This is a natural extension of Gibson's notion of object affordance (Gibson, 1977) to functional and goal-directed aspects of Generative Lexicon's Qualia Structure (Pustejovsky, 2013; Pustejovsky and Krishnaswamy, 2021), and is situationally grounded within a semantically interpreted 4D simulation environment (temporally interpreted 3D space), called VoxWorld (McNeely-White et al., 2019; Krishnaswamy et al., 2022).

VoxML has also been proposed for annotating visual information as part of the ISO 24617 series of international standards on semantic annotation schemes, such as ISO-TimeML (ISO, 2012) and ISO-Space (ISO, 2020). VoxML, as an annotation language, should be specified in abstract terms, general enough to be interoperable with other annotating languages, especially as part of such ISO standards, while licensing various implementations in concrete terms. In order to address these requirements, this paper aims to formulate an abstract syntax of VoxML based on a metamodel. It develops as follows: Section 2, Motivating VoxML as an Annotation Language, Section 3, Specification of an Annotation Scheme, based on VoxML, Section 4, Interpretation of Annotation-based Logical Forms with respect to the VoxML Minimal Model, and Section 5, Concluding Remarks.

2 Motivating VoxML as an Annotation Language

Interpreting actions and motions requires situated background information about their agents or related objects, occurrence conditions, and enriched lexical information. The interpretation of base annotation structures, anchored to lexical markables for annotating visual perceptions, depends on various sorts of parametric information besides their associated dictionary definitions.

A significant part of any model for situated com-

[1] VoxML represents a *visual object concept structure (vocs)* modeling language.

Proceedings of the 19th Joint ACL - ISO Workshop on Interoperable Semantic Annotation, pages 66–74
June 20, 2023.

munication is an encoding of the semantic type, functions, purposes, and uses introduced by the "objects under discussion". For example, a semantic model of perceived *object teleology*, as introduced by Generative Lexicon (GL) with the Qualia Structure, for example, (Pustejovsky, 1995), as well as *object affordances* (Gibson, 1977) is useful to help ground expression meaning to speaker intent. As an illustration, consider first how such information is encoded and then exploited in reasoning. Knowledge of objects can be partially contextualized through their *qualia structure* (Pustejovsky and Boguraev, 1993), where each Qualia role can be seen as answering a specific question about the object it is bound to: *Formal*, the IS-A relation; *Constitutive*, an object PART-OF or MADE-OF relation; *Agentive*, the object's CREATED-BY relation; and *Telic*: encoding information on purpose and function (the `used-for` or FUNCTIONS-AS relation).

While such information is needed for compositional semantic operations and inferences in conventional models, it falls short of providing a representation for the *situated grounding* of events and their participants or of any expressions between individuals involved in a communicative exchange. VoxML provides just such a representation. It further encodes objects with rich semantic typing and action affordances and actions themselves as multimodal programs, enabling contextually salient inferences and decisions in the environment. To illustrate this, consider the short narrative in (1) below.

(1) Mary picked up the glass from the table and put it in the dishwasher to wash and dry it.

VoxML provides the means to better interpret these events as situationally grounded in interactions between an agent and objects in the world.

In order to create situated interpretations for each of these events, there must be some semantic encoding associated with how the objects relate to each other physically and how they are configured to each other spatially. For example, if we associate the semantic type of "container" with glass, it is situationally important to know how and when the container capability is activated: i.e., the orientation information is critical for enabling the use or function of the glass *qua* container. VoxML encodes these notions that are critical for Human-Object Interaction as: *what* the function associated with an object is (its affordance), and just as critically, *when* the affordance is active (its habitat). It also explicitly encodes the dynamics of the events bringing about any object state changes in the environment, e.g., change in location, time, and attribute.

3 Specification of the Annotation Scheme

3.1 Overview

VoxML is primarily a modeling language for simulating actions in the visual world. Still, it can also be used as a markup language for (i) annotating linguistic expressions involving human-object interactions, (ii) translating annotation structures in shallow semantic forms in typed first-order logic, and then (iii) interpreting with the minimal model simulated by VoxML by referring to the voxicon, or set of voxemes, as shown in Figure 1.

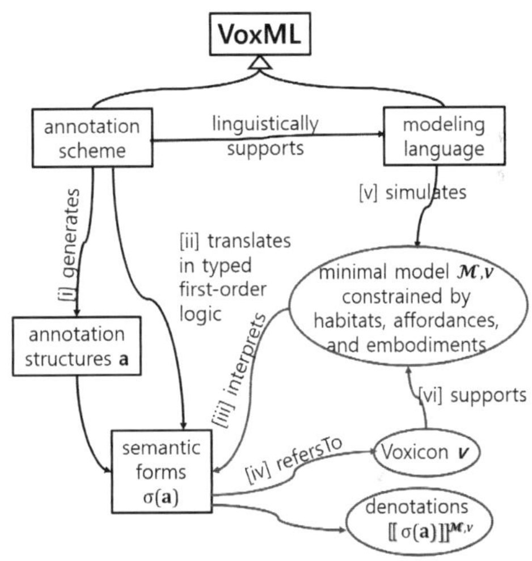

Figure 1: How VoxML operates

This section formally specifies the VoxML-based annotation scheme, with a metamodel (3.2), an abstract syntax (3.3), a concrete representation of annotation structures (3.4), and their translation to semantic forms in typed first-order logic (3.5).

3.2 Metamodel of the VoxML-based Annotation Scheme

A metamodel graphically depicts the general structure of a markup language. As pointed out by Bunt (2022), a metamodel makes the specification of annotation schemes intuitively more transparent, thus becoming a *de facto* requirement for constructing semantic annotation schemes. The metamodel, represented by Figure 2, focuses on interactions between entities (objects) and humans, while the *dynamic paths*, triggered by their actions, trace the visually perceptible courses of those actions. The VoxML-based annotation scheme, thus represented, is construed to annotate linguistic expressions for human-object interactions (cf. Henlein et al. (2023)).

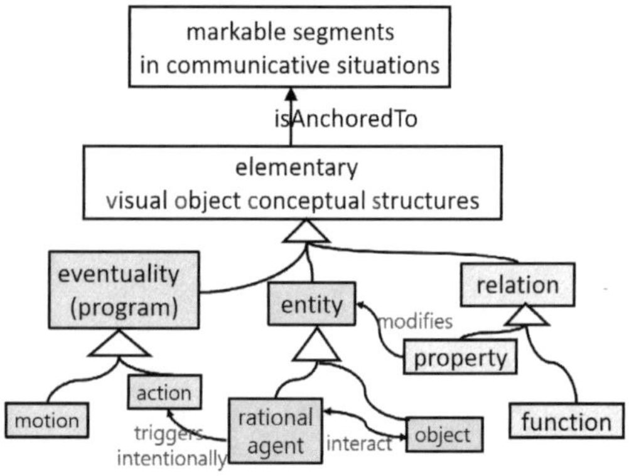

Figure 2: Metamodel of VoxML

We view the VoxML model or world as inhabited by only three categories of entities: *event (program):action*, *object*, and *relation*. Each of them has subcategories, as represented by the hollow triangles in Figure 2.[2] Because of its key role in VoxML, category *action* is introduced as a subcategory of category *event*. This model represents a *small minimal* world, focused on actions, (physical) objects, and their interrelations, which together constitute the larger ontology such as SUMO (Niles and Pease, 2001). Unlike other types of eventuality, agents intentionally trigger actions, and these agents can be humans or other rational agents. These agents also interact with objects as participants in actions.

Category *relation* has two subcategories, *property* and *function*. As unary relations, properties modify entities (objects), as in *big table*. Functions are particular relations mapping one object to another. The function *loc* for *localization*, for instance, maps physical objects (e.g., *table*) to spatial locations where some other objects like apples can be placed. As introduced by Katz (2007), the runtime function τ maps eventualities to times such that $\tau(e)$ refers to the occurrence time of the event e. We may also introduce a function *seq* that forms paths by ordering pairs $t@l$ of a time t and a location l. The VoxML annotation language has no category such as location, time, or path, but can introduce time points to discuss, for instance, their temporal ordering: e.g., $\tau(e_1) \prec \tau(e2)$. Binary or any other n-ary relations, such as *in* or *between*, are of category *relation* and are also introduced into VoxML.

VoxML, as a modeling language, views physical objects and actions as forming visually perceptible conceptual structures called *voxemes*. Applied to language and its constituent expressions, the VoxML-based annotation scheme takes them as *markables*, anchored to a word, an image, a gesture, or anything from communicative actions that consist of verbal descriptions, gestures, and surrounding backgrounds.

3.3 Abstract Syntax

An abstract syntax defines a specification language and rigorously formulates its structures. In constructing natural language grammars (Lee, 2016, 2023), the abstract syntax of a semantic annotation scheme is defined as a tuple in set-theoretic terms. The abstract syntax $\mathcal{AS}yn_{voxml}$ of the VoxML-based annotation scheme is also defined as a set-theoretic tuple, as in Definition 2:

(2) Definition of $\mathcal{AS}yn_{voxml}$:
Given a finite set D, or data, of communicative segments in natural language, the abstract syntax $\mathcal{AS}yn_{voxml}$ of VoxML is defined to be a triplet $<M, C, @>$, where:

- M is a nonnull subset of D that contains (possibly null or non-contiguous) strings of communicative segments, called *markables*, each delimited by the set B of base categories.
- C consists of base categories B and relational categories R:
  - Base categories B and their subcategories, as depicted in Figure 2: [i] *event:action*, [ii] *entity (object)* and [iii] *relation*:{*property*, *function*}.
  - Relational categories R: unspecified for $\mathcal{AS}yn_{voxml}$.
- $@_{cat}$ is a set of assignments from attributes to values specified for each category cat in C.

For every base category cat in B, the assignment $@_{cat}$ has the following list of attributes as required to be assigned a value:

(3) **Assignment** $@_{cat}$ in Extended BNF:
```
attributes =
identifier, target, type, pred;
identifier = categorized prefix
  + a natural number;
target = markable;
type = CDATA;
pred = CDATA|null;
  (* predicative content *)
```

[2]In UML, a hollow triangle represents a subcategorization relation.

Each category may have additional required or optional attributes to be assigned a value. For instance, the assignment $@_{action}$ is either a *process* or *transition* type. Category *action* has the attribute `@agent`, which triggers it.

3.4 Representing Annotation Structures

The annotation scheme, such as $\mathcal{AS}_{voxml}$, generates annotation structures based on its abstract syntax. These annotation structures have two substructures: *anchoring* and *content* structures. In pFormat[3], these two structures are represented differently by representing anchoring structures by their values only, but content structures as attribute-value pairs.

The first part of Example (1) is annotated as follows:

(4) a. Base-segmented Data:
Mary$_{x1,w1}$ picked up$_{e1,w2-3}$ the glass$_{x2,w5}$ from$_{r1,w6}$ the table$_{x3,w8}$.

b. Annotation Structures:
object`(x1, w1,`
`type="human", pred="mary")`
action`(e1, w2-3,`
`type="transition", pred="pickUp",`
`agent="#x1", physObj="#x2")`
object`(x2, w5,`
`type="physobj", pred="glass")`
relation`(r1, w6,`
`type="spatial", source="#x3")`
object`(x3, w8,`
`type="physobj", pred="table")`

In base-segmented data, each markable is identified by its anchoring structure $<cat_i, w_j>$ (e.g., `x1, w1`), where cat_i is a categorized identifier and w_j is a word identifier. The agent which triggered the action of picking up the glass is marked as Mary$_{x1}$, and the object glass$_{x2}$ is related to it.

Interoperability is one of the adequacy requirements for an annotation scheme. Here, we show how the VoxML-based annotation scheme is interoperable with other annotation schemes, such as ISO-TimeML (ISO, 2012) and the annotation scheme on anaphoric relations (see Lee (2017) and ISO (2019)). The rest of Example (1) can also be annotated with these annotation schemes. It is first word-segmented, while each markable is tagged with a categorized identifier and a word identifier as in (5):

(5) a. Primary Data:
Mary picked up the glass from the table and put it in the dishwasher to wash and dry it.

b. Base-segmented Data:
Mary$_{x1,w1}$ [picked up]$_{e1,w2-3}$ the glass$_{x2,w5}$ from$_{r1,w6}$ the table$_{x3,w8}$ and put$_{e2,w10}$ it$_{x4,w11}$ in$_{r2,w12}$ the dishwasher$_{x5,w14}$ to wash$_{e3,w16}$ and dry$_{e4,w18}$ it$_{x6,w19}$.

Second, each markable is annotated as in (6):

(6) Elementary Annotation Structures:
action`(e2, w10`
`type="transition", pred="put"`
`agent="#x1", relatedTo="#x4")`
object`(x4, w11,`
`type="unknown", pred="pro")`
relation`(r2, w12`
`type="spatial", pred="in")`
object`(x5, w14,`
`type="physobj, artifact",`
`pred="dishwasher")`
action`(e3, w16,`
`type="process", pred="wash",`
`agent="#5, theme="#x6")`
action`(e4, w18,`
`type="process", pred="dry",`
`agent="#x5", theme="#x6")`
object`(x6, w19,`
`type="unknown", pred="pro")`

The first two actions *pick up* and *put* are triggered by the human agent *Mary*, whereas the actions of *wash* and *dry* are triggered by the dishwasher, which is not human.

The annotation scheme $\mathcal{AS}_{voxML}$ for actions annotates the temporal ordering of these four actions by referring to ISO-TimeML, as in (7):

(7) a. Temporal Links (`tLink`):
tLink`(tL1, eventID="#e2",`
`relatedToEventID="#e1",`
`relType="after")`
tLink`(tL2, eventID="#e3",`
`relatedToEventID="#e2",`
`relType="after")`
tLink`(tL3, eventID="#e4",`
`relatedToEventID="#e3",`
`relType="after")`

[3] pFormat is a predicate-logic-like annotation format for replacing XML, thus being constrained to introduce embedded structures into annotations.

b. Semantic Representation:
$[pickUp(e_1), put(e_2), wash(e_3), dry(e_4), \tau(e_1) \prec \tau(e_2) \prec \tau(e_3) \prec \tau(e_4)]$[4]

The annotation scheme $\mathcal{AS}_{voxML}$ can also refer to the subordination link (`sLink`) in ISO-TimeML (ISO, 2012) to annotate subordinate clauses such as *to wash and dry it* in Example (1).

(8) a. Subordination Link (`sLink`):

sLink`(sL1, eventID="#e2", relatedTo="{#e3,#e4}", relType="purpose")`

b. Semantic Representation:
$[put(e_2), wash(e_3), dry(e_4), purpose(e_2, \{e_3, e_4\})]$

The subordination link (8) relates the actions of *wash* and *dry* to the action of *put* by annotating that those actions were the *purpose* of *putting* the glass in the dishwasher.

By referring to the annotation schemes proposed by Lee (2017) or ISO (2019), the VoxML-based annotation scheme can annotate the anaphoric or referential relations involving pronouns. The two occurrences of the pronoun *it* refer to the noun *the glass* are annotated as in (9):

(9) a. Annotation of Coreferential Relations:

object`(x2, w5, type="physobj, artifact", pred="glass")`
anaLink`(aL1, x4, x2, identity)`
anaLink`(aL2, x6, x2, identity)`

b. Semantic Representation:
(i) $\sigma(x2) := [glass(x_2)]$,
$\sigma(aL1) := [x_4{=}x_2]$,
$\sigma(aL2) := [x_6{=}x_1]$
(ii) $[glass(x_2), x_4{=}x_2, x_6{=}x_2]$

Semantic Representation (ii) is obtained by unifying all the semantic forms in (i). It says that the two occurrences of the pronoun *it* both refer to the glass.

3.5 Annotation-based Semantic Forms

The annotation scheme translates each annotation structure $\mathbf{a}_4$ into a semantic form $\sigma(\mathbf{a}_4)$, as in (10).

(10) a. Base Semantic Forms σ:[5]
$\sigma(x1) := \{x_1\}[human(x_1), mary(x_1)]$
$\sigma(x2) := \{x_2\}[physObj(x_2), glass(x_2)]$
$\sigma(x3) := \{x_3\}[physObj(x_3), table(x_3)]$
$\sigma(e1) := \{e_1\}[action(e_1), transition(e_1), pickUp(e_1), agent(e_1, x_1), theme(e_1, x_2)]$
$\sigma(r1) := \{r_1\}[relation(r_1), source(r_1, x_3)]$

b. Composition of the Semantic Forms:
$\sigma(\mathbf{a}_4) := \oplus\{\sigma(x1), \sigma(x2), \sigma(x3), \sigma(e1), \sigma(r1)\}$

By unifying all of the semantic forms in (10a), we obtain the semantic form $\sigma(\mathbf{a_1})$ of the whole annotation structure $\mathbf{a}_1$. This semantic form roughly states that Mary picked up a glass (see $\sigma(e1)$), which moved away from the table. This interpretation is too shallow to view how Mary's picking up the glass from the table happened. It was on the table, but now it is no longer there. It is in the hand of Mary, who grabbed it. It didn't move by itself, but its location followed the path of the motion how Mary's hand moved.

3.6 Interpreting Annotation-based Semantic Forms

To see the details of the whole motion, as described by Example (1a), we must know the exact sense of the verb *pick up*. WordNet Search - 3.1 lists 16 senses, most rendered when the verb is used with an Object as a transitive verb. Picking up a physical object like a glass or a book means taking it up by hand, whereas picking up a child from kindergarten or a hitchhiker on the highway means taking the child home or giving the hitchhiker a ride. Such differences in meaning arise from different agent-object interactions. The VoxML-based annotation scheme refers to Voxicon that consists of voxemes and interprets the annotation-based semantic forms, such as (10), with respect to a VoxML model.

4 Interpretation with respect to the VoxML Minimal Model

Voxemes in VoxML create a minimal model. Each of the annotation-based semantic forms, as in (10),

[4]These semantic forms can be represented in DRS validly. See Lee (2023).

[5]As noted earlier, DRS (Kamp and Reyle, 1993) represents these semantic forms in an equivalent way.

is interpreted with respect to this minimal model by referring to its respective voxemes.

4.1 Interpreting Objects

There are four objects mentioned in Example (1): $mary(x_1)$, $glass(x_2)$, $table(x_3)$, and $dishwasher(x_5)$.[6] The semantics forms in (10) say very little. For instance, the semantic form $\sigma(x2)$ of the markable *glass* in (10) says it is a *physical object* but nothing else.

In addition to the lexical information, as given by its annotation structure and corresponding semantic form, each entity of category *object* in VoxML is enriched with information with the elaboration of [i] its *geometrical type*, [ii] the *habitat* for actions, [iii] the *affordance structures*, both Gibsonian and telic, and [iv] the agent-relative *embodiment*.

In a voxicon, such information is represented in a typed feature structure. An example is given in Figure 3 for the object *glass*.[7]

$$
\begin{bmatrix}
\textbf{glass} \\
\text{LEX} = \begin{bmatrix} \text{PRED} = \textbf{glass} \\ \text{TYPE} = \textbf{physobj, artifact} \end{bmatrix} \\
\text{TYPE} = \begin{bmatrix} \text{HEAD} = \textbf{cylindroid[1]} \\ \text{COMPONENTS} = \textbf{surface, interior} \\ \text{CONCAVITY} = \textbf{concave} \\ \text{ROTATSYM} = \{Y\} \\ \text{REFLECTSYM} = \{XY, YZ\} \end{bmatrix} \\
\text{HABITAT} = \begin{bmatrix} \text{INTR} = [2] \begin{bmatrix} \text{CONSTR} = \{Y > X, Y > Z\} \\ \text{UP} = align(Y, \mathcal{E}_Y) \\ \text{TOP} = top(+Y) \end{bmatrix} \\ \text{EXTR} = [3] \begin{bmatrix} \text{UP} = align(Y, \mathcal{E}_{\perp Y}) \end{bmatrix} \end{bmatrix} \\
\text{AFFORD\_STR} = \begin{bmatrix} A_1 = H_{[2]} \rightarrow [put(x, on([1]))]support([1], x) \\ A_2 = H_{[2]} \rightarrow [put(x, in([1]))]contain([1], x) \\ A_3 = H_{[2]} \rightarrow [grasp(x, [1])] \\ A_4 = H_{[3]} \rightarrow [roll(x, [1])] \end{bmatrix} \\
\text{EMBODIMENT} = \begin{bmatrix} \text{SCALE} = \textbf{<agent} \\ \text{MOVABLE} = \textbf{true} \end{bmatrix}
\end{bmatrix}
$$

Figure 3: VoxML representation for object *glass*

The TYPE structure in Figure 3 contains definitions of rotational symmetry ROTATSYM and reflectional symmetry REFLSYM. The rotational symmetry ROTATSYM of a shape gives the major axis of an object such that when the object is rotated around that axis for some interval of less than or equal to 180 °, the shape of the object looks the same. Examples of shapes with rotational symmetry are *circle*, *triangle*, etc. The reflectional symmetry REFLSYM is a type of symmetry which is with respect to reflections across the plane defined by the axes listed, e.g., a *butterfly* assuming vertical orientation would have reflectional symmetry across the YZ-plane.

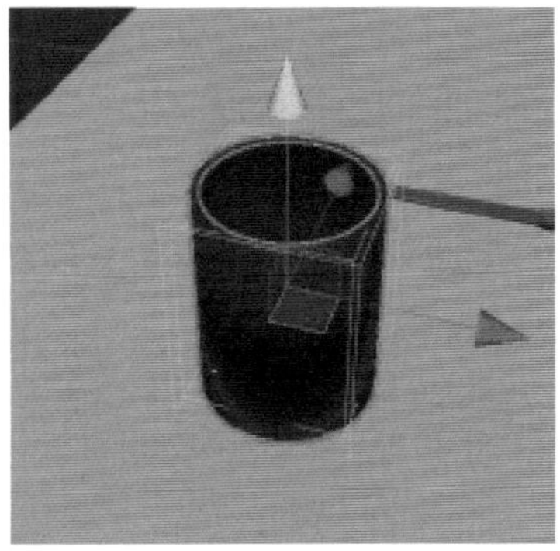

Figure 4: Rendering of object *glass* (cf. Figure 3) showing orthogonal axes.

Figure 4 shows a 3D rendering of a glass object as defined by the structure Figure 3, taken from the VoxWorld platform (Pustejovsky et al., 2017; Krishnaswamy et al., 2022). The object is shown with the 3 major orthogonal axes of the 3D world The green axis is the Y-axis, which is the axis of rotational symmetry. The glass is also symmetric across the XY-plane (defined by red and green axes) and the YZ-plane (defined by the green and blue axes).

Under the HABITAT structure in Figure 3, the variables X, Y, and Z correspond to extents in standard Cartesian coordinates, representing the dimensions, such as areas, required to represent 3D objects in space. From these areas, the radii or circumferences of the bottom and the top areas and the height of the glass are obtainable. Note that the top of a glass has its top area open as a container. Unlike the solid cylindroid, the glass consists of two sheets for the closed bottom and the side such that the circumference of the top area only stands for the width of the side sheet. Note also that the size of the circumference of the top Y, which is the brim of a glass, may equal or be larger than that of the bottom X.

The *habitat* describes environmental and configurational constraints that are either inherent to the object ("intrinsic" habitats, such as a glass having an inherent top, regardless of its placement in the environment), or required to execute certain activ-

[6]The variables x_4 and x_6 are assigned to the two occurrences of the pronoun *it*.

[7]Taken from the Voxicon in Krishnaswamy and Pustejovsky (2020).

ities with it ("extrinsic" habitats, such as a glass needing to be placed on its side to be rollable).

This representation provides the necessary information for its full interpretation. It says the object is glass, a physical artifact having the shape of a concave cylindroid and other geometrical features. It should be standing concave upward to hold liquid. Thus, it can be placed on the table, contain water or wine, and be grasped by a hand. It may roll if it falls sideways, but it does only if it does not have something like a handle or is not designed like a wine glass. The embodiment says it is smaller than the one holding it and can move.

4.2 Interpreting Agents

A voxeme for an agent may refer to an actual human agent or an AI agent of any form (humanoid, robotic, or without distinct form). Other entities, or rational agents, may function as agents as long as they are capable of executing actions in the world (Krishnaswamy, 2017; Pustejovsky et al., 2017) Examples developed using the VoxWorld platform include collaborative humanoid agents that interact with humans and objects, including interpreting VoxML semantics in real time to exploit and learn about object affordances (Krishnaswamy et al., 2017, 2020; Krishnaswamy and Pustejovsky, 2022), navigating through environments to achieve directed goals (Krajovic et al., 2020), and also self-guided exploration where the VoxML semantics "lurk in the background" for the agent to discover through exploratory "play" (Ghaffari and Krishnaswamy, 2022, 2023). The physical definition of agents conditions their actions (Pustejovsky and Krishnaswamy, 2021). For instance, a humanoid agent with defined *hand* $\sqsubseteq_c$ *arm* $\sqsubseteq_c$ *torso* is enabled to execute the act of grasping, while a robotic agent defined with *wheels* $\sqsubseteq_c$ *chassis* $\sqsubseteq_c$ *self* is enabled for the act of locomotion. This has implications for the semantics of how the agent is interacted with: the humanoid can *pick up* objects while the robot can *go to* them.

4.3 Interpreting Actions as Programs

Actions are viewed as *programs* that can formally implement them as processes, (dynamic) sequences of sub-events or states, recursions, algorithms, and execution (see Mani and Pustejovsky (2012) and de Berg et al. (2010)).

The voxemes for actions are much simpler than those for objects. They consist of three attributes: [i] Lex for lexical information, [ii] Type for argument structure, and [iii] Body for subevent structure. The information conveyed by [i] and [ii] is provided by the annotation structures for predicates with their attributes @type, @pred, @agent, and @physObj.

(11) Annotation Structure:
action`(a1, w2-3,`
`type="transition", pred="pickUP",`
`agent="#x1", physObj="#x2")`

As being of type *transition*, the action of picking up involves two stages of a motion, [i] the initial stage of *grasping* the glass and [ii] the ensuing process of *moving* to some direction while *holding* it. This involvement is stated by part of the voxeme for the predicate *pick up*, as in (12):[8]

(12) Embodiment for *pick up*:
a. $E_1 = grasp(x, y)$
b. $E_2 = [while(hold(x, y), move(x, y, vec(\mathcal{E}_Y)))]$

The embodiment E_2 states that the agent x moves the glass y, as her hand and arm move together, along the path or vector $\mathcal{E}_Y$ while holding it (see Harel et al. (2000) for *while* programs or *tail recursion*).

4.4 Interpreting the Role of Relations

The preposition *from* functions as a spatial relation between the object *glass* and the table on which it was located and supported. Then, as the hand of the agent *Mary* holding the glass moves, the glass is no longer on the table but moves away along the path that the hand moves. Hence, the relation *from* marks the initial point of that path or vector.

5 Concluding Remarks

The paper specified the VoxML-based annotation scheme in formal terms. The example of the action of Mary picking up a glass from the table showed how that particular example was annotated and how its logical forms were interpreted with a VoxML model while referring to the voxicon. Each voxeme in the Lexicon, especially that of objects, contains information enriched with the notions of habitat, affordance, and embodiment. As the voxicon develops into a full scale, the task of interpreting

[8]This information is derived from the voxeme for *lift* in Krishnaswamy and Pustejovsky (2020) and applied to the predicate *pick up*.

annotated language data involving complex interactions between humans and objects can easily be managed.

For purposes of exposition, the discussion here focused on the annotation of one short narrative in English involving one verb, *pick up*, and one object, *glass*. The proposed VoxML-based annotation scheme needs to be applied to large data with a great variety to test the effectiveness of interpreting its annotation structures and corresponding semantic forms against the VoxML model. At the same time, such an application calls for the need to enlarge the size and variety of the voxicon for modeling purposes as well. The evaluation of the VoxML-based annotation scheme and the extension of the voxicon remain as future tasks.

Acknowledgments

This paper has been revised with the constructive comments from four reviewers. We thank them all for their suggestions.

References

Harry Bunt. 2022. Intuitive and formal transparency in semantic annotation schemes. In *Proceedings of the 18th Joint ACL-ISO Workshop on Interoperable Semantic Annotation (ISA-18)*, pages 102–109, Workshop at LREC2022, Marseilles, France.

Mark de Berg, Otfried Choeng, Marc van Kreveld, and Mark Overmars. 2010. *Computational Geometry: Algorithms and Applications*. Springer, Berlin. Third Edition.

Sadaf Ghaffari and Nikhil Krishnaswamy. 2022. Detecting and accommodating novel types and concepts in an embodied simulation environment. In *Proceedings of the Tenth Annual Conference on Advances in Cognitive Systems*.

Sadaf Ghaffari and Nikhil Krishnaswamy. 2023. Grounding and distinguishing conceptual vocabulary through similarity learning in embodied simulations. In *Proceedings of the 15th International Conference on Computational Semantics*. ACL.

James Jerome Gibson. 1977. The theory of affordances. *Perceiving, Acting, and Knowing: Toward an Ecological Psychology*, pages 67–82. Reprinted as chapter 8 of Gibson (1979).

David Harel, Dexter Kozen, and Jerzy Tiuryn. 2000. *Dynamic Logic*. The MIT Press, Cambridge, MA.

Alexander Henlein, Anju Gopinath, Nikhil Krishnaswamy, Alexander Mehler, and James Pustejovksy. 2023. Grounding human-object interaction to affordance behavior in multimodal datasets. *Frontiers in Artificial Intelligence*, 6(1084740):01–12. Doi:10.3389/frai.2023.1084740.

ISO. 2012. *ISO 24617-1 Language resource management – Semantic annotation framework – Part 1: Time and events*. International Organization for Standardization, Geneva.

ISO. 2019. *ISO 24617-9 Language resource management – Semantic annotation framework – Part 9: Reference annotation framework (RAF)*. International Organization for Standardization, Geneva.

ISO. 2020. *ISO 24617-7 Language resource management – Semantic annotation framework – Part 7: Spatial information*. International Organization for Standardization, Geneva. 2nd edition.

Hans Kamp and Uwe Reyle. 1993. *From Discourse to Logic: Introduction to Model-theoretic Semantics of Natural Language, Formal Logical and Discourse Representation Theory (Studies in Linguistics and Philosophy)*. Kluwer, Dordrecht.

Graham Katz. 2007. Towards a denotational semantics for TimeML. In Frank Schilder, Graham Katz, and James Pustejovsky, editors, *Annotation, Extracting, and Reasoning about Time and Events*, pages 88–106. Springer, Berlin.

Katherine Krajovic, Nikhil Krishnaswamy, Nathaniel J Dimick, R Pito Salas, and James Pustejovsky. 2020. Situated multimodal control of a mobile robot: Navigation through a virtual environment. *RoboDial*.

Nikhil Krishnaswamy. 2017. *Monte Carlo Simulation Generation Through Operationalization of Spatial Primitives*. Ph.D. thesis, Brandeis University.

Nikhil Krishnaswamy, Pradyumna Narayana, Rahul Bangar, Kyeongmin Rim, Dhruva Patil, David McNeely-White, Jaime Ruiz, Bruce Draper, Ross Beveridge, and James Pustejovsky. 2020. Diana's world: A situated multimodal interactive agent. In *Proceedings of the AAAI Conference on Artificial Intelligence*, 34.9, pages 13618–13619.

Nikhil Krishnaswamy, Pradyumna Narayana, Isaac Wang, Kyeongmin Rim, Rahul Bangar, Dhruva Patil, Gururaj Mulay, Ross Beveridge, Jaime Ruiz, Bruce Draper, et al. 2017. Communicating and acting: Understanding gesture in simulation semantics. In *IWCS 2017–12th International Conference on Computational Semantics–Short papers*.

Nikhil Krishnaswamy, William Pickard, Brittany Cates, Nathaniel Blanchard, and James Pustejovsky. 2022. The VoxWorld platform for multimodal embodied agents. In *Proceedings of the Thirteenth Language Resources and Evaluation Conference*, pages 1529–1541.

Nikhil Krishnaswamy and James Pustejovsky. 2020. VoxML specification 1.0. *Unpublished*.

Nikhil Krishnaswamy and James Pustejovsky. 2022. Affordance embeddings for situated language understanding. *Frontiers in Artificial Intelligence*, 5.

Kiyong Lee. 2016. An abstract syntax for ISO-Space with its <moveLink> reformulated. In *Proceedings of the 12th Joint ACL-ISO Workshop on Interoperable Semantic Annotation (ISA-13)*, pages 107–118, Workshop at the 12th International Conference on Computational Semantics (IWCS 2017), Montpellier, France.

Kiyong Lee. 2017. Semantic annotation of anaphoric links in language. *Linguistics and Literature Studies*, 5.4:248–270. DOI: 10.131189/lls.2017.050403.

Kiyong Lee. 2023. *Annotation-Based Semantics for Space and Time in Language.* Cambridge University Press, Cambridge, UK.

Inderjeet Mani and James Pustejovsky. 2012. *Intepreting Motion: Grounded Representation for Spatial Language.* Oxford University Press, Oxford.

David G McNeely-White, Francisco R Ortega, J Ross Beveridge, Bruce A Draper, Rahul Bangar, Dhruva Patil, James Pustejovsky, Nikhil Krishnaswamy, Kyeongmin Rim, Jaime Ruiz, et al. 2019. User-aware shared perception for embodied agents. In *2019 IEEE International Conference on Humanized Computing and Communication (HCC)*, pages 46–51. IEEE.

Ian Niles and Adam Pease. 2001. Toward a standard upper ontology. In *Proceedings of the 2nd International Conference on Formal Ontology in Information Systems (FOIS-2001).* Ogunquit, Maine.

James Pustejovsky. 1995. *The Generative Lexicon.* The MIT Press, Cambridge, MA.

James Pustejovsky. 2013. Dynamic event structure and habitat theory. In *Proceedings of the 6th International Conference on Generative Approaches to the Lexicon (GL2013)*, pages 1–10. Association for Computational Linguistics, Pisa, Italy.

James Pustejovsky and Olga Batiukova. 2019. *The lexicon.* Cambridge University Press.

James Pustejovsky and Bran Boguraev. 1993. Lexical knowledge representation and natural language processing. *Artificial Intelligence*, 63:193–223.

James Pustejovsky and Nikhil Krishnaswamy. 2016. VoxML: A visualization modeling language. In *Proceedings of the Tenth International Conference on Language Resources and Evaluation (LREC'16)*, pages 4606–4613, Portorož, Slovenia. ELRA. ACL anthology L16-1730.

James Pustejovsky and Nikhil Krishnaswamy. 2021. Embodied human-computer interaction. *KI-Künstliche Intelligenz*, 35(3-4):307–327.

James Pustejovsky, Nikhil Krishnaswamy, and Tuan Do. 2017. Object embodiment in a multimodal simulation. In *AAAI Spring Symposium: Interactive Multisensory Object Perception for Embodied Agents.*

How Good is Automatic Segmentation as a Multimodal Discourse Annotation Aid?

Corbyn Terpstra, Ibrahim Khebour, Mariah Bradford, Brett Wisniewski, Nikhil Krishnaswamy and Nathaniel Blanchard
Department of Computer Science
Colorado State University
Fort Collins, CO, USA
{cytoniv,nblancha}@colostate.edu

Abstract

Collaborative problem solving (CPS) in teams is tightly coupled with the creation of shared meaning between participants in a situated, collaborative task. In this work, we assess the quality of different utterance segmentation techniques as an aid in annotating CPS. We (1) manually transcribe utterances in a dataset of triads collaboratively solving a problem involving dialogue and physical object manipulation, (2) annotate collaborative moves according to these gold-standard transcripts, and then (3) apply these annotations to utterances that have been automatically segmented using toolkits from Google and OpenAI's Whisper. We show that the oracle utterances have minimal correspondence to automatically segmented speech, and that automatically segmented speech using different segmentation methods is also inconsistent. We also show that annotating automatically segmented speech has distinct implications compared with annotating oracle utterances—since most annotation schemes are designed for oracle cases, when annotating automatically-segmented utterances, annotators must invoke other information to make arbitrary judgments which other annotators may not replicate. We conclude with a discussion of how future annotation specs can account for these needs.

1 Introduction

In order for Artificially Intelligent (AI) agents to interact with with an environment, they must first accurately perceive that environment. In real-world contexts, this necessitates automatically preprocessing various modalities for downstream procedures. For example, an AI agent to modulate classroom discourse needs to first identify distinct discourse components, but a single spoken utterance from a team member could contain multiple discourse components. The identification of each discourse component within the utterance could easily spiral into a doctoral thesis but overly fixating on this preprocessing step would make it extremely difficult to make substantive progress on AI agents themselves.

Typically, researchers default to "oracle" data, where one assumes the preprocessing step has been completed with human level accuracy (e.g., human transcriptions of speech, utterances segmented by dialogue move). However, in a real-world agent deployment, preprocessing of data that would be fed into the automated system will instead be handled by off-the-shelf software. Current practice in AI assumes the existence of suitable datasets that contain examples of the information an automated system is intended to extract. The task of developing the AI model entails solving for the function that best maps from the input samples to the desired outputs. If these datasets do not already exist, then the information that is to be learned must be annotated by humans.

Consider the scenario we focus on in this paper: a group collaborating to solve a problem involving the shared manipulation of physical objects. Multiple modalities are implicated in such a task—group members speak to each other, but also point or gesture, use body language, and manipulate objects to communicate meaning and intent. Specs intended for annotating *collaborative problem solving* (CPS) skills on display are intended to be used at the utterance level, and assume that the utterance has been segmented and transcribed by humans ("oracles"). There are many frameworks for modeling CPS that have been developed by researchers in the learning sciences (e.g., Roschelle and Teasley (1995); Cukurova et al. (2018); Andrews-Todd and Forsyth (2020); Sun et al. (2020)) and this literature stresses the multimodal nature of CPS (Dillenbourg and Traum, 2006). For example, the occurrence of an interruption or the content of cross-talk may not be immediately evident from the audio signal

Proceedings of the 19th Joint ACL - ISO Workshop on Interoperable Semantic Annotation, pages 75–81
June 20, 2023.

alone, but watching the speakers interact may make it clear who is speaking when or what is said. High-quality annotation of oracle utterances of a multimodal task like CPS therefore relies on annotators attending to the multiple modalities implicated while making their decisions. If the annotations are performed without this information, or with this information scrambled somehow, we should expect this to affect the quality of the annotation. The question is, how much?

The development of such annotation schemes is typically conducted separately from the rapid preprocessing and scaling that AI practitioners are likely to encounter when they use such annotated data for model training. There may be little that AI practitioners can ask of spec developers given the risk involved with the development of an annotation spec (one can imagine the truly unpleasant experience of developing an annotation spec and finding, after innumerable modeling and annotation cycles, that meaning captured in the spec is not linked to the expected meaningful outcomes). Further, spec developers may (arguably rightly) say that they have no expectation that their spec will be used to train AI models, and that the problems that unfold should be solved by AI developers themselves. These are quite reasonable arguments—and unless the annotation spec is being explicitly developed for AI systems, annotators are unlikely to change (we strongly encourage annotations developed for AI to think deeply about these problems—but such thoughts are outside of the scope of this particular paper). Nonetheless, AI development relies on interoperable annotated data, and as AI practitioners ourselves, we conclude that AI practitioners must think deeply about traditional annotation schemes and how we can best accommodate them.

In this paper, the annotation scheme we use is the one developed by Sun et al. (2020) but the problem we address is independent of any particular spec. Namely, when an annotation spec designed for one utterance segmentation method is applied to utterances automatically segmented using a different method, the information retrieved is different from what the original spec intended to encode.

We annotate utterances for CPS using expert annotators, and we also have expert annotators label, as best they can, automatically-segmented utterances. We discuss common strategies to transfer oracle annotations to real-world annotations. We underscore, exactly, how disconnected the oracle utterance labels may be from the labels on automatically-segmented utterances. Finally, we discuss how, given even just two automatic utterance segmentation methods, achieving a gold-standard annotating become quickly intractable if the specification itself does not contain strategies for accommodating suboptimal preprocessing.

2 Related Work

The gap between oracle data and real-world data has been identified previously (Blanchard et al., 2016). Other works have pointed out the need to move away from oracle transcriptions in pursuit of AI applications for real-world use cases (Morbini et al., 2013; Blanchard et al., 2018). The use of automatic segmentation of speech for modeling tasks is becoming increasingly widespread (Bradford et al., 2022a,b; Castillon et al., 2022).

Modeling in general has become more aware of the needs of real-world systems. For example, methods for automatically detecting mind wandering have moved from balanced datasets to heavily imbalanced datasets in acknowledgement of the need for such models to operate in the context of real-world distributions (Kuvar et al., 2022).

What is distinct with this work is that here we focus our analysis on the annotation implications, rather than on attempts to fix issues that arise through machine learning directly. For example, Blanchard et al. (2018) refused to use human transcriptions in a multimodal sentiment challenge because such transcripts were not true to real-world contexts; however, they did not comment on how the labeling of sentiment might change were those annotations done on automatically extracted data.

Here, we explicitly focus on that challenge. We explore the implications of segmentation and transcription methods when annotating CPS for groups. CPS is a critical skill used in many areas of life (Graesser et al., 2018), and AI agents for group settings will need some way of representing group state. Work has been done to model CPS at the utterance level (Stewart et al., 2021; Bradford et al., 2023). The framework defined by Sun et al. (2020) captures CPS at three levels and identifies specific actions that indicate different types of collaborative actions and their impact on group state. In particular, we hope our efforts here facilitate consistency across future CPS modeling efforts and meaningfully contribute to the CPS framework defined by Sun et al. (2020), and in general, we hope to prompt thought about annotation spec design and strategy in the face of potential uses involving automated preprocessing.

3 Dataset

Our dataset consists of audiovisual recordings of 10 triads performing a shared collaborative task which was developed to promote rich collaboration via multimodal communication. The task is performed by triads at a round table in a laboratory setting. The equipment on the table includes 6 blocks (of varying weight, size, and color), a balance scale, a worksheet demarcated with spaces to place the blocks (indicated with weights in grams), and a laptop on which participants submit their responses to survey questions throughout the task.

Participants are first given a balance scale to determine the weights of five of the colored wooden blocks. They are told that one block weighs 10 grams, but that they have to determine the weights of the rest of the blocks using the balance scale.[1] As the weight of each block is determined, participants place it on the worksheet next to its corresponding weight. The participants also must submit their final answer for the weight of each block to the survey form on the laptop. Once the weights of all five blocks are solved for, participants are given the sixth block and must identifying its weight *without* using the scale (i.e., participants have to deduce the weight based on the pattern observed in the initial block weights). Finally, participants are asked to determine the weight of another mystery block that is *not physically present* and explain how they arrived at the answer. The participants once again submit their answer as a group in the online survey and are given two chances (with a hint after the first guess if it is incorrect).

The total dataset consists of 10 videos, containing 3 participants each, for a total of 170 minutes of video. Participants ranged from 19–35 years old, recruited from a university population. 20% were female while 80% were male. 60% were Caucasian non-Hispanic, 10% were Hispanic/Latino, and 30% were Asian. All volunteers spoke English through the task but spoke a variety of native languages.

Although this data was collected in a lab, the complexity of human-human interaction is appropriately captured in these recordings — participants talk over each other, they speak with disfluencies, they interrupt each other, they engage in long run-on sentences punctuated by only a single em-dash, and they pause in the middle of sentences before resuming their thought. All of these complications make utterance segmentation quite difficult, and often these ambiguities are only resolved by human annotators with recourse to the visual modality.

4 Preprocessing

4.1 Automatic Segmentation of Speech

Automatic Speech Recognition, or ASR, approaches, must necessarily determine the boundaries of utterances. Each ASR model segments audio in unique ways. This can be either through waiting for any pause in the audio, or waiting until a break of a certain length is encountered. ASR allows for AI to break apart the speech for the listener to in principle break down the amount of empty noise within audio recordings, and different systems using the same ASR component are interoperable on this level.

4.2 Whisper

Whisper (Radford et al., 2022) is a speech recognition system developed by OpenAI that was trained on 680,000 hours of audio to accurately determine and transcribe speech across many different languages. Whisper takes audio files and will listen to the first 30 seconds, or less depending on the length of the file, to determine the language of the speech. It will then segment the audio into full second segments, and will rarely cut off before a single or multiple full seconds have passed. Whisper is also optimized to segment audio into full sentences instead of simply looking for a break in the audio. In principle, this allows for transcription of long audio segments (e.g., lectures or speeches) with a fidelity closer to human transcription.

4.3 Google ASR

Google ASR (Velikovich et al., 2018) is a speech recognition system released by Google, Inc. Google ASR listens for what it assumes to be human speech and attempts to transcribe what it hears. Google also will attempt to segment audio wherever it finds a break in speech. If a word is not picked up by the microphone correctly or is slightly inaudible, then Google will cut off the word and move on with the next segmentation. This could mean cutting off a thought mid-sentence, or removing words entirely from what someone is saying.

5 Annotation Methodology

Videos were first hand-transcribed to ensure the accuracy of the transcriptions. These hand, or ora-

[1]The pattern to the weights of the blocks is based on the Fibonacci sequence.

cle transcriptions, were then measured against the transcriptions from both Google ASR and Whisper.

5.1 Annotation Procedure

When annotating the oracle files, speech start and end times would be marked down to the hundredth of a second. Each audio file would then be segmented into proper sentences or thoughts if the sentences were not completed. If people within the audio recording spoke over each other, each person's sentence was recorded as closely as possible, each with its own beginning and ending timestamp. This was done for each audio file from the 10 separate groups. Each segmented utterance was then coded by expert annotators using an updated version of the framework developed by Sun et al. (2020). The annotators initially annotated all 10 videos separately, to get familiar with the framework, then were trained by experts in the framework on one video, while discussing how each CPS indicator would align with the weights task. The experts then annotated another video with a Fleiss' kappa score of 0.62 (agreement over 96% of the number of subjects to be coded).

6 Transferring Annotations from Oracle to Automatically-Segmented Utterances

Once oracle utterances are labeled, we map those labels to the automatically segmented utterances. The approach for that mapping depends on the task at hand and the type of labels we see. In the case of labeling collaborative problem solving (CPS), the multiclass binary labels can be inherited from the oracle segments to the automatic segments using overlap in timestamps. This is because the labels all still exist during that period. However, we lose label accuracy when we lose the exact timestamp where the label occurred. Another option is to only apply labels that occur in every oracle included in the segment; however, with CPS, this would rarely occur and we would lose most of our labels.

7 Effects of Oracle vs. Automatic Utterance Segmentation

Count of utterances Table 1 shows the different number of utterances segmented out by each method for each group.

Almost uniformly, Whisper segments more individual utterances than occur in the oracle transcripts, due to breaking up single oracle utterances into multiples (exceptions are groups 7 and 10). Across all groups, Google segmentation creates fewer (sometimes far fewer) utterances than exist

Group	1	2	3	4	5	6	7	8	9	10
Whisper	297	201	391	293	406	278	311	354	136	346
Google	139	151	254	128	146	153	380	235	90	146
Oracle	229	207	337	195	237	227	590	338	134	379

Table 1: # of utterances per group determined by each segmentation method. Totals: Whisper - 3,013 utterances; Google - 1,822 utterances; Oracle - 2,873.

in the oracle, due to dropping utterances entirely or mistaking speech for background noise. Google ASR does perform very well removing empty space from audio files compared to Whisper.

Intrinsic ASR metrics Evaluation of the automatic speech transcription itself after automatic segmentation can be used as a proxy for information lost in part due to the segmentation process. Since error rates must be calculated with respect to the same set of utterances in order to be directly comparable, we focused this analysis on the transcription of Google-segmented utterances. Given an oracle transcript with assumed insertion, deletion, substitution, and total word error rates of 0, we observe that while overall word error rate (WER) is similar using Google and Whisper (Google: 0.573; Whisper: 0.542), Google has higher rates of substitutions (words in the oracle swapped for a different word) and deletions (words in the oracle removed by automated transcription), while Whisper has a significantly higher rate of insertions (words in the automated transcript not in the oracle). See Table 2.

We investigated why Whisper had far more insertions and found it was linked to Google utterances that did not contain any speech. Occasionally, when listening to the audio files Google will hear empty noise as speech and create a segment for it. When feeding Whisper an audio segment containing only background noise, it would generate its own sentence to fill the void, and would occasionally choose a random language to generate the utterance in as well. This does not pose an issue in most situations, since the main purpose of ASR and transcription software would be to transcribe and recognize actual speech in audio files. Thus, the WER of Whisper seems to be partially be a product of our decision to use Google utterances. An appropriate method to filter out such segments, or, the use of Whisper's own segmentation would likely substantially lower the WER of whisper.

We also noticed Whisper would insert words when there was no speech recognized in the audio

	Google				Whisper			
Group	WER	Sub. rate	Del. rate	Ins. rate	WER	Sub. rate	Del. rate	Ins. rate
1	0.571	0.252	0.113	0.206	0.534	0.193	0.045	0.296
2	0.459	0.211	0.128	0.120	0.416	0.177	0.040	0.200
3	0.539	0.236	0.117	0.186	0.527	0.177	0.047	0.303
4	0.529	0.267	0.154	0.170	0.572	0.201	0.040	0.332
5	0.631	0.262	0.173	0.195	0.581	0.175	0.060	0.346
6	0.581	0.252	0.077	0.252	0.525	0.191	0.041	0.293
7	0.610	0.260	0.155	0.196	0.650	0.209	0.064	0.377
8	0.532	0.259	0.137	0.137	0.486	0.200	0.048	0.238
9	0.571	0.274	0.180	0.118	0.514	0.229	0.084	0.202
10	0.645	0.306	0.087	0.252	0.612	0.202	0.054	0.356
Average	0.573	0.259	0.132	0.183	0.542	0.195	0.052	0.294

Table 2: WER, substitution rate, deletion rate, and insertion rate by group.

clip. Typically words that had been previously transcribed would be repeated during void sections, and only one word or phrase would be repeated. This word or phrase would also be repeated for each second during the break, which created a large amount of insertions and threw off some data while testing. Finally, we found Google ASR would also hear words incorrectly and misinterpret what the speaker was saying, replacing the intended words with homonyms or phonological near-neighbors.

Difference in resulting annotation labels The difference in labels when going from automatic segments to oracle segments can be significant. A particular case is the annotation of interruptions, one of the CPS indicators in question. Relying on the automatic segments only may split or lump utterances separated by an interruption, which may cause annotators to miss the interruption entirely (because they are only coding utterance by automatically segmented utterance), or lumping an "interruption" annotation with annotations of other meaningful indicators in a single, multi-speaker "utterance." For tasks like this, each utterance is important as it can be the one where the correct solution has been proposed. Interestingly, Bradford et al. (2023) found that prosodic features were essential for identifying interruptions when using automatically segmented utterances, indicating there may be times automatic segmentation methods capture information not present in oracle contexts.

One example of label difference can be seen in the utterances shown in Fig. 1, with the different segmentations provided by oracle and automatic segmentation. The utterances "Weren't those both

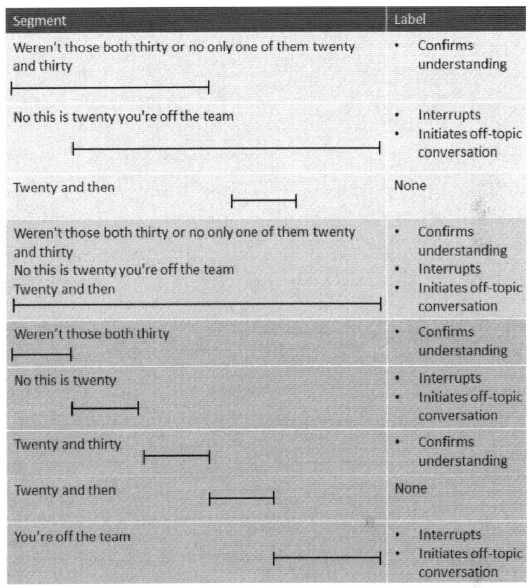

Figure 1: Overlap between oracle (top), Google (middle), and Whisper (bottom) segments. Right column shows the CPS indicator annotated for each utterance.

thirty or no only one of them twenty and thirty", "No this is twenty you're off the team" and "Twenty and then" (which were each spoken by a different person), are combined into one segment by Google voice activity detection (VAD). The first utterance should have the label *confirms understanding*, the second utterance should have the labels *interrupts* and *initiates off-topic conversation*, and the third utterance should have no label. However, when these are combined, all of the labels are inherited and the distinction between the different content supplied by each utterance is lost. Whisper segments split up continuous utterances by a single person, and thus person 2's *interrupts* and *initiates off-topic conversation* indicators are applied to two separate segments. Both of these cases can cause confusion in downstream semantic classification tasks like classifying CPS indicators from linguistic features, as in Bradford et al. (2023), if the target label for training is not clear.

In some instances, the participant pauses mid-sentence and the true utterance gets split into two, but for lack of context only one gets assigned a CPS indicator. For example, a participant says "Think it just feels like it's," pauses for 0.3 seconds, and says, "A lot heavier because it's denser and like just carrying that.", the whole sentence should get coded as *discussing results*, but since the automatic segmentation splits the sentence into two utterances, only the second utterance would be coded as such.

8 Discussion, Recommendations, and Conclusion

One important point to emphasize is the manual cost of annotating for collaborative problem solving (CPS). CPS is a difficult annotation scheme to master (training can last as long as 6 months, depending on how much time a coder is putting toward learning). Although this paper largely focuses on the automated processes of segmenting audio, annotations themselves require complete multimodal context including viewing of video, listening to intonation, and the inclusion of temporal context. If these annotations, performed with access to multimodal information, are subsequently applied to automatically-segmented audio, then the information lost can be expected to impact downstream tasks trained or evaluated over the annotated data, thus potentially wasting the time taken to train annotators properly.

While automatic segmentation of utterances for various semantic annotation tasks certainly saves time and annotator effort, it comes at a potentially significant cost to the quality of annotations for downstream tasks. Particularly, automatic segmentation and transcription methods certainly segment utterances differently from a human oracle transcriber, and different ASR methods perform segmentation drastically differently with profoundly divergent results. This may result in utterances being missed by the automatic segmenter or invented out of whole cloth, which would cause annotators annotating at the automatically-segmented utterance level to likewise omit annotations, or to encounter "hallucinated" segments that are either un-annotatable or, if annotated, introduce semantic noise into the data. Beyond the obvious, we have shown that annotating at the oracle utterance level but then transferring those utterances to the automatically-segmented utterance level may obscure the semantic information originally captured at the oracle utterance level. Even taking the more labor-intensive step of generating oracle transcriptions before annotating is less useful if annotation is not performed at the same level. This backs up previous conclusions in semantic annotation over text-only corpora, such as the need for annotators to come to consensus on both spans and annotations (Pustejovsky and Stubbs, 2012), and shows that they also apply to multimodal use cases.

However, as multimodal AI develops and becomes more integrated with everyday life, inference will necessarily be performed over automatically segmented and transcribed inputs. Therefore, future models will benefit from annotation specs themselves that are task-aware and can take into account potential noise introduced by imperfect automated transcription and adjust accordingly. For instance, if multiple labels are not allowed, should certain labels "dominate" others in case multiple labels are squeezed into the same segment? Future semantic annotation schemes, specifications, and languages, particularly over multimodal data, will need to take into account these requirements to more effectively use automated techniques like ASR as part of larger annotation and inference pipelines.

Acknowledgments

We would like to thank our reviewers for their helpful comments. This work was supported in part by the United States National Science Foundation (NSF) under grant number DRL 2019805 to Colorado State University. The views expressed are those of the authors and do not reflect the official policy or position of the U.S. Government. All errors and mistakes are, of course, the responsibilities of the authors.

References

Jessica Andrews-Todd and Carol M. Forsyth. 2020. Exploring social and cognitive dimensions of collaborative problem solving in an open online simulation-based task. *Computers in human behavior*, 104:105759.

Nathaniel Blanchard, Patrick J. Donnelly, Andrew M. Olney, Borhan Samei, Brooke Ward, Xiaoyi Sun,

Sean Kelly, Martin Nystrand, and Sidney K. D'Mello. 2016. Semi-automatic detection of teacher questions from human-transcripts of audio in live classrooms. *International Educational Data Mining Society*.

Nathaniel Blanchard, Daniel Moreira, Aparna Bharati, and Walter Scheirer. 2018. Getting the subtext without the text: Scalable multimodal sentiment classification from visual and acoustic modalities. In *Proceedings of Grand Challenge and Workshop on Human Multimodal Language (Challenge-HML)*, pages 1–10.

Mariah Bradford, Paige Hansen, J. Ross Beveridge, Nikhil Krishnaswamy, and Nathaniel Blanchard. 2022a. A deep dive into microphone hardware for recording collaborative group work. In *Proceedings of the 15th International Conference on Educational Data Mining*, page 588.

Mariah Bradford, Paige Hansen, Kenneth Lai, Richard Brutti, Rachel Dickler, Leanne Hirshfield, James Pustejovsky, Nathaniel Blanchard, and Nikhil Krishnaswamy. 2022b. Challenges and opportunities in annotating a multimodal collaborative problem-solving task. In *Interdisciplinary Approaches to Getting AI Experts and Education Stakeholders Talking Workshop, AIEd*.

Mariah Bradford, Ibrahim Khebour, Nathaniel Blanchard, and Nikhil Krishnaswamy. 2023. Automatic detection of collaborative states in small groups using multimodal features. In *Proceedings of the 124th International Conference on Artificial Intelligence in Education*.

Iliana Castillon, Videep Venkatesha, Hannah VanderHoeven, Mariah Bradford, Nikhil Krishnaswamy, and Nathaniel Blanchard. 2022. Multimodal features for group dynamic-aware agents. In *Interdisciplinary Approaches to Getting AI Experts and Education Stakeholders Talking Workshop, AIEd*.

Mutlu Cukurova, Rose Luckin, Eva Millán, and Manolis Mavrikis. 2018. The NISPI framework: Analysing collaborative problem-solving from students' physical interactions. *Computers & Education*, 116:93–109.

Pierre Dillenbourg and David Traum. 2006. Sharing solutions: Persistence and grounding in multimodal collaborative problem solving. *The Journal of the Learning Sciences*, 15(1):121–151.

Arthur C. Graesser, Stephen M. Fiore, Samuel Greiff, Jessica Andrews-Todd, Peter W. Foltz, and Friedrich W. Hesse. 2018. Advancing the Science of Collaborative Problem Solving. *Psychological Science in the Public Interest*, 19(2):59–92. Publisher: SAGE Publications Inc.

Vishal Kuvar, Nathaniel Blanchard, Alexander Colby, Laura Allen, and Caitlin Mills. 2022. Automatically detecting task-unrelated thoughts during conversations using keystroke analysis. *User Modeling and User-Adapted Interaction*, pages 1–25.

Fabrizio Morbini, Kartik Audhkhasi, Kenji Sagae, Ron Artstein, Doğan Can, Panayiotis Georgiou, Shrikanth Narayanan, Anton Leuski, and David Traum. 2013. Which asr should i choose for my dialogue system? In *Proceedings of the SIGDIAL 2013 Conference*, pages 394–403.

James Pustejovsky and Amber Stubbs. 2012. *Natural Language Annotation for Machine Learning: A guide to corpus-building for applications.* " O'Reilly Media, Inc.".

Alec Radford, Jong Wook Kim, Tao Xu, Greg Brockman, Christine McLeavey, and Ilya Sutskever. 2022. Robust speech recognition via large-scale weak supervision. *arXiv preprint arXiv:2212.04356*.

Jeremy Roschelle and Stephanie D. Teasley. 1995. The construction of shared knowledge in collaborative problem solving. In *Computer supported collaborative learning*, pages 69–97. Springer.

Angela E. B. Stewart, Zachary Keirn, and Sidney K. D'Mello. 2021. Multimodal modeling of collaborative problem-solving facets in triads. *User Modeling and User-Adapted Interaction*, 31(4):713–751.

Chen Sun, Valerie J. Shute, Angela Stewart, Jade Yonehiro, Nicholas Duran, and Sidney D'Mello. 2020. Towards a generalized competency model of collaborative problem solving. *Computers & Education*, 143:103672. Publisher: Elsevier.

Leonid Velikovich, Ian Williams, Justin Scheiner, Petar S. Aleksic, Pedro J. Moreno, and Michael Riley. 2018. Semantic lattice processing in contextual automatic speech recognition for google assistant. In *Interspeech*, pages 2222–2226.

Author Index